THE SEO WAY

Search Engine Optimization for Beginners

By Tarek Riman

"Marketing works holistically and not one thing at a time."

This book goes to my family, my friends, the hard-working entrepreneurs, the believers, the dreamers, the students and the fighters.
Never. Give. Up.

To God & The Universe *for blessing me with this journey, this book, and every breath.*

Published by
Cap.TaiM Marketing Inc.
captaim.com
ISBN: 9781073695164

Cover photos & cover design by Nancy Morris
Edits by Melissa Dawn and Erin Lariviere

DISCLAIMER
This book is designed to provide information, motivation and empowerment to readers. It is sold with the understanding that the author is not assured to deliver any kind of psychological advice (e.g. legal, medical, psychological) or be a substitute for professional assistance. No warranties or guarantees are expressed or implied by the writer in the content of this volume. The author shall not be liable for any physical, psychological, emotional, financial or commercial damages, including, but not limited to, special, incidental, consequential or other damages. The reader is responsible for their own choices, actions, and results. Situations, people and context have been changed as appropriate to protect the privacy of others.

Tarek Riman
Visit my website at https://captaim.com/the-seo-way/

Printed in the United States of America

First Printing: July 2019
Cap.TaiM Marketing Inc.

ISBN: 9781073695164

A Quick Introduction

The purpose of *The SEO Way* is to help start-ups, students, companies, beginners and entrepreneurs bring value to their websites and online properties through Search Engine Optimization, aka SEO.

SEO is the practice of aligning the structure, content and other strategies and elements of a web property with the rules and best practices of the search engines that hold so much influence over the web (e.g. Google and Bing).

Every business or individual with a web presence needs SEO to improve their site's chances of appearing on search engine results pages and being found by their target audience.

In this book, I provide a simple and accessible introduction to SEO: what it's all about, the rules that govern it, its evolution and how it works with every other aspect of digital marketing.

This book will give you the tools and foundational knowledge you need for your SEO to be successful and impactful. As you go through it, remember that SEO does not work on its own. It works best when combined with analytics, coding, keywords, content and more. These will all be outlined within this book to help you approach SEO in a holistic way to drive real results.

TABLE OF CONTENTS

Introduction

The Vision Behind the Book

To help, to inspire, to motivate and to support.

As I travel and work, I run into a lot of people around the world who are struggling with over complicated marketing ideas.

The goal of this book is to make sure that any business owner, student or marketer that picks up this book is able to immediately familiarize themselves with the concepts and begin using them to their advantage.

Disclaimer

In this book, as in life, there are no guarantees.

As the title indicates, this book is for beginners. It is intended to help people who are new to the field of SEO easily understand and capitalize on SEO strategies and best practices to bring their brands to the next level.

Its purpose is to help get you started on SEO and to guide you to an understanding of how you can use it to your advantage in digital marketing and web strategies.

The majority of the profits from this book will go to support refugees, as well as education and child-related charities.

To stay posted on which charities we will be supporting, please visit our website: https://captaim.com/the-seo-way/

Glossary

Glossary of Terms

2xx status code - A code indicating success in retrieving the correct response to a request. This (and other status codes) happens in the background of your website. 2xx status codes are an indication that your site code is functioning well, elements are loading properly and users are able to efficiently navigate and interact with your site.

301 redirect - This is a permanent redirect that signals search engines that a webpage has permanently moved to a new location/URL, and directs the engines to the new location. This type of redirect allows the SEO strength of an old page to be maintained and carried over to its new location.

302 redirect - This is a temporary redirect that signals search engines that a webpage and/or its contents has temporarily moved to a new location. This is problematic for SEO as the search engine then has to decide which page to keep - the original, or the new location. There aren't many instances where you would temporarily move a webpage, so why would someone do this? From a technical perspective, a 302 redirect is easier to set up than a 301. If you don't have SEO in mind, a 302 can be tempting, as the user experience is the same either way. This is a good example of why SEO needs to be considered any time an onsite change is made.

3xx status code - These status codes indicate a redirect to search engines and browsers. 301 redirect is an example of a 3xx status code. See also "301 redirect".

4xx status code - These are typically error codes such as the "404 Not Found" or "408 Request Timeout" errors you may sometimes come across when browsing the web.

5xx status code - Indicates a server error. "500 Internal Server Error" is one example. If you come across a 5xx error on your own site, that tells you the problem is with the server.

Actionable insight - Any insight upon which you can take action. This is one of the main benefits of tools like Google Analytics - to extract insight or knowledge that you can then act on to improve your business or marketing efforts.

AMP - Stands for Accelerated Mobile Pages. It is a type of simplified coding language that loads much faster on mobile devices. It is a Google-backed project and is open source, meaning it is available to anyone to use.

Algorithm - An algorithm is sometimes simplified as a formula for solving a problem. That's part of it, but an algorithm can actually be either a formula or a procedure. It's purpose is to solve a problem and it does so by following a very specific sequence of actions. Search engine algorithms solve the problem of retrieving and ranking the information that best suits the user's search query. As technology evolves, and the wealth of data about users (their habits, preferences, interests, etc.) grows, these algorithms become more and more complex.

Alt tag - An alt tag is descriptive text about an image on a webpage. These alt tags are used by screen reading software to make the internet more accessible to the visually impaired community. They are also read by search engines. Search engines can't reliably "read" images (yet), but they can recognize when an image is present in the site code and they look for the alt tag to understand what the image is all about.

Analytics - Analytics is the link between raw data and data-driven decision making. It is the process of aggregating, displaying and communicating data in a way that reveals meaningful patterns, with the intention of using those patterns to make stronger, knowledge-based decisions for your business.

Anchor text - This is the clickable text you see on webpages. When you want to link a bit of text to another webpage (for example, "Learn more by visiting our product page."), you add a hyperlink to that text. The user doesn't see the actual link or the bits of code that make it clickable. Instead they see the text, usually in blue font and underlined, indicating that it is clickable. This is called the anchor text.

Average position - The average position of your web property in search engine results pages (see also "SERP").

Backlinks - Links from other sites linking into your website. In general, backlinks help build the SEO strength of your site, as search engines see them as an indicator that the linked-to site is valuable in some way. The exception is when a backlink has a "nofollow" attribute. See "Do-follow link" and "No-follow link" below.

Behaviours - The actions people take on your web property, or on the internet in general. A behaviour can be scrolling, clicking, searching, entering information, watching a video, navigating to various pages, etc. It is how people interact with the internet or your web property.

Behavioural marketing - The process of marketing to specific behaviours. In this type of marketing, rather than deliver the same message or content to all users, you tailor content to specific behaviours. For example, you may create specific content for certain search terms, for return visitors, for shoppers who have items in their cart but have not checked out, etc.

Black hat - This is an SEO approach that goes against search engine rules, regulations and general best practices in an attempt to "trick" search engines and rig search engine results pages. It sometimes leads to short term gains in terms of ranking positions, but search engine technology today is intelligent enough to quickly flag these bogus results and will often penalize sites for using such tactics. That can be extremely difficult to come back from. Black hat tactics also rarely provide any real value to users, so while search rankings may jump, it rarely leads to any significant or sustainable increase in overall business success. See also "White hat".

Blogging platform - A service used for blogging. Examples include Wordpress and Tumblr.

Bot - "Bot" can mean many things, but when it comes to search engines, a bot is a program that crawls websites and pages across the web, indexing the content and returning that data to search engines to be ranked and categorized for users. Search engine bots are sometimes called crawlers.

Bounce - When a visitor to your web property leaves the site without ever taking any action.

Brand awareness - The level of audience recognition of your brand name, logo, tagline or other brand-specific elements. It can also refer to the likelihood that someone will think of your brand when faced with the problem you solve or gap you fill.

Branded term - A search term that includes the name of your brand or business.

Caching - The practice of temporarily storing information on a device's memory. For example, when you go to a website that you visit often and the website address auto fills after typing just one or two letters, that's because the information has been temporarily stored in your cache.

Call to action (CTA) - A direction or invitation to site visitors to take a specific action. Examples include: buy now, sign up here, reserve your spot, download your free eBook, watch this video, etc.

Canonical tag - This tag tells search engines which page is the original source - the canon. Canonical tags are a method of eliminating duplicate content, as duplicate content can dilute page strength and hinder SEO efforts. If your site has both an http and https version, for example, you can use canonical tags to ensure the https version is seen as canonical and the http version is not considered duplicate content.

Channels - Essentially, a pathway. For the purposes of this book, a channel can be the pathway taken by customers to get to your website (clicking on an ad or search result can be a channel), or it can be the pathway through which you promote your products or services (newsletters, ads, social media, etc.).

Click - When a user or visitor clicks on something. Depending on what you are tracking, this can be a click on a paid ad, a link on social media, an email or newsletter click, a click on a link within your site, etc.

Click through rate - The ratio of people who click a link over the number of people who view the page, ad, email, SERP, etc. For example, if 1,000 people see your AdWords ad and 10 of those people click on the ad, you would calculate 10/1,000x100 = 1, giving you a 1% click through rate.

Cloaking - This is the practice of showing one version of a webpage to users and another to search engines. It is typically used as a tactic for tricking search engines and rigging rankings. Although it has a few, outdated valid uses, it is mainly a black hat SEO tactic and can get your site penalized by search engines. See also "Black hat".

Content - Content is everything your visitors see or hear. Content can be copy, video, audio and images. Even quizzes or questionnaires can be considered content. It is what you put out there for your audience to consume.

Copy - Written words. Your copy is the text on your website, blog, newsletters, etc.

Conversion - A conversion is anytime a customer or site visitor completes a desired action on your web property. Conversions will differ from business to business, depending on your unique goals and objectives. Examples of conversions include a sale, newsletter sign up, app download, event registration, etc. The action must be fully completed to be considered a conversion.

Conversion rate - The percentage of visitors to your site or web property who complete a specific goal or objective. See "Conversion" above.

Creative - Another word for the graphic imagery used in marketing or advertising. The visual element of a newsletter, for example, may be referred to as the "creative".

Dashboard - A user interface that displays the most important information in a quick, easy-to-read fashion. An analytics dashboard, for example, is ideally laid out to show you your most critical stats and trends, immediately. Deep dives into data take place beyond the dashboard.

Data - In Google Analytics, data is the collected statistics and facts about your website or web properties, user behaviour and demographics, market trends, etc. It is the raw information. On its own, it is simply too much information for humans to identify meaningful patterns and trends. Analytics is the organization of that data into something meaningful and readable. See "Analytics" above.

Data-driven strategy - Marketing or business strategies driven by data. For example, instead of assuming that holidays will mean a boost in sales, we look to the data to see exactly when traffic, search or interest begins to rise, what specific terms are being used, who our audience is, etc., then we build marketing strategies off of that knowledge and insight.

Data hygiene - The practice of ensuring data is as "clean" as possible, meaning we are not collecting duplicate data, incomplete data, outdated data or otherwise compromised data. From a dashboard and reporting perspective, it is the practice of ensuring your visual data is clutter-free and easy to read. See "Dashboard" above.

Data source - The source of your information. For example, if you have connected Google Analytics and Google AdWords, when you view data from AdWords within Analytics, AdWords is your data source.

De-index - The practice of instructing search engine bots not to index a particular page. The bots can still crawl the page, but cannot add it to the search engine's index. This is accomplished by implementing a "noindex" tag. Common uses of the "noindex" tag include confirmation pages (confirmation of a newsletter signup, for example) or on printer-friendly versions of pages. This allows search engine bots to focus on the more important pages and can prevent duplicate content. See also "Bots".

Demographics - Population based factors such as geographical location, age, language, gender, religion, education, etc.

Development environment - A server for development purposes only. The content on this server is never made public. It is where developers build, test and debug new software, features, fixes or versions of a website or application.

Device - The physical product used by someone to access your site or web property. Examples of devices include laptop or desktop computers, smartphones and tablets.

Digital marketing - All marketing conducted and consumed in the digital realm.

Do-follow link - When one site links to another site, it is an indicator to search engines that the linked-to site is valuable in some way, and can help strengthen that site's SEO. The site doing the linking generally gains and loses nothing by having the link, so long as the link is also relevant to their own content, making it a good way for the internet community to support each other and support good content. You can manually add the "dofollow" attribute to specific links or entire pages but, unless otherwise specified, all links are generally considered "dofollow" by search engines, whether they have the attribute or not. See "No-follow links" below.

Domain authority - A ranking system developed by Moz to predict how well a website will rank in SERPs. See also "Search engine results pages (SERP)".

Domain hosting - Your domain is the address of your website, for example, http://caminowithin.com is a domain. Registering your domain with a domain hosting provider is like registering your physical address - it allows your address to exist, essentially. This is different from web hosting. A web hosting service hosts all of your site content, structure, security measures, etc. It is usually a good idea to have your domain and web hosting handled by separate companies. This way, if you ever have an issue with your web hosting company and want to switch, that company has no hold over your domain name, making it a lot easier for you to make the change while maintaining your domain name.

Duplicate content - This is when you have the exact same content at two or more different URLs. A common example is when you have "www" and "non-www" versions of your website. Search engines see them as two different sites and will count all the content as duplicate. This dilutes the SEO strength of your content because search engines have to figure out which page to give value to. Two methods of solving the duplicate content issue are 301 redirects and canonical tags. See also "301 redirect" and "Canonical tags".

Ecommerce - The practice of selling products or services online. An ecommerce site is a site that sells something.

Email marketing - The practice of promoting products or services, building brand awareness or conducting any other marketing activity through email. Typically, email newsletter subscribers are gathered through online forms, at points of sale, or some other method of email collection. However, emails such as registration confirmations, order receipts, etc. can sometimes include marketing elements and, therefore, fall under the umbrella of "email marketing".

Engagement - When a brand and consumer connect in a meaningful way. Engagement on a website is often measured by time spent on site, or number of actions taken on a site. It is when a visitor discovers content that holds their attention and keeps them interested.

Exit - When someone leaves your site or web property. They may close the app or web browser, or leave to go to another site.

External linking - A link from one domain/site to a different domain/site. See also "Backlinks" and "Link building".

External site - This usually refers to linking. When another website (for example a blog or online magazine) links to your website, you would say the traffic from that link is coming from an external site. Essentially, it is any website outside of your network. See also "External linking".

GDPR (General Data Protection Regulation) - Regulation adopted by the EU concerning data privacy. The regulation applies to businesses located outside the EU as well, if they intend to do business within the EU. To learn more, visit www.gdpr.associates.

Gmail - Google's free email service. To use any Google service, you first need a Gmail account.

Google Analytics - Web analytics service that tracks website or mobile app traffic and behaviour, and presents it in readable report formats.

Google AdWords - Online advertising platform where advertisers bid on keywords and phrases to have their ads displayed alongside search results and websites within the Google advertising network.

Google Data Studio - Google Data Studio is all about the aesthetics of reporting. It allows you to create reports and dashboards that are easy to read and easy to understand. You can also add branding and other personalization elements to reports in GDS.

Google Insights - A Google service that provides insight into people's search behaviour and preferences. It does not provide any personally identifiable information. Instead, it shows search trends by date, geographical location and demographic information.

Google My Business listing - This listing allows you to create an eye-catching and useful business listing that will appear when people search for your business on Google or on Google Maps. You can provide details about your business including directions, price range, website, etc., as well as interact with your customers in the comments.

Google Optimize - A Google tool that allows you to run tests on your website, emails, app or other digital properties to determine the best performing elements.

Google Search Console - This tool allows you to see how your site is performing from a search perspective. What keywords are people using to find you? Where is your site showing up in search results pages? How often are people clicking on your search results? You can find all that through GSC.

Google Trends - This tool gives you insight into search trends. You can use it to identify seasonal spikes or slumps in searches for your brand, related brands, your products or services, etc.

Guest blogging - The practice of writing articles for publishing on another person or company's blog, but attributed to you or your company as the author. Usually, guest blogging is a two-way street, where each party creates a post for the other party's blog. By doing so, each party can potentially increase traffic to their own site, increase brand awareness, boost their domain authority and build on their link building efforts. It's also a great way of building relationships. Typically, people or businesses within the same industry or field will engage in guest blogging, but not direct competitors. See also "Domain authority" and "Link building".

Header tags - These tags are used to indicate main headings (h1 tag) and subheadings (tags h2-h6), and to differentiate them from the rest of the content. From an SEO perspective, these headers give structure to your site and make it more readable, which both users and search engines appreciate.

HTML - Stands for Hypertext Markup Language. It is a computer language used for creating websites and applications.

Image title tag - When you hover your cursor over an image on a webpage, a little text blurb usually pops up. This is an image title tag.

Implementation - From a marketing perspective, implementation is the process of actually putting a marketing campaign live and into action. It is the actual sending of newsletters, putting new content live, posting to social media, etc.

Impressions - Anytime your content is displayed on a screen. This could be a webpage, an ad, an embedded video, etc. Each display of the content is considered an impression.

Intent - In marketing, when we talk about intent, we're talking about the user's intention when they take an action. For example, if someone looks up "dry cleaner" in a Google search, their intention is most likely to find dry cleaning services near them. They probably aren't looking for the dictionary definition of "dry cleaner" or the history of dry cleaning. Intent matters because giving people what they want is how businesses thrive, and how we build strong SEO.

Internal linking - The practice of linking from one page within your site to another page within your site. The most common way of doing this is through a sitemap, as well as through your site's navigation menus. Internal linking is part of your site's structure and is important for both users and search engines, as it helps both to easily and efficiently navigate your site.

Keywords - The words and phrases people enter into search engines when looking for products, services, information, etc.

Keyword density - The percentage of times keywords appear on a page relative to the overall page content. There is no magic number, however, a very high keyword density may be an indicator to search engines of keyword stuffing, which search engines do not view favorably. Instead of focusing on density, aim to have your primary and secondary keywords appear in the first paragraph of your content and ensure it is written in a useful and natural way that makes sense for the user. See also "Keyword stuffing".

Keyword difficulty - Also called keyword competition. The higher the difficulty of a keyword, the more difficult it will be to achieve the #1 ranking spot in search engine results pages, and the greater the competition from other sites to do so. See also "Search engine results pages (SERPs).

Keyword stuffing - The practice of jamming as many keywords, and/or as many instances of specific keywords, into a page or site as possible. This is a black hat technique and generally frowned upon by search engines. It may result in a short-term bump in search rankings, but will not provide long term results and may get your site penalized by search engines. See "black hat" below.

KPI - Key performance indicator. Many organizations use KPIs either instead of, or in addition to, goal setting as a means of measuring performance of a team, individual, project, initiative, etc.

Landing page - The specific page a visitor lands on when they first arrive at your site. For example, if someone on your company Facebook page clicks a link to your latest blog post, the blog post they arrive at is their landing page.

Leads - A lead is collected contact information of someone who is not yet a customer, but may become one. A newsletter subscriber is one example. This person has not yet purchased from you, but you now have their email address and permission to contact them, which you can then use to market products and services in hopes of converting them to a customer.

Link building - When evaluating the quality and/or relevancy of a website, one of the things search engines take into account is the external site (See "External site" above) linking to yours. Having several links from other reputable sites that direct to your site boosts the validity of your site in the eyes of search engines. Link building is the practice of actively seeking out external links to your site. One common way of doing this is by providing content (articles, videos, etc.) to external blogs or online magazines that link back to your website. It can be a time consuming and lengthy process, and takes dedication, but the payoff is big. Not only do search engines see these links favourably, but they also increase brand awareness and often send high quality traffic your way. See also "Backlinks" and "External links".

Load time - The time it takes for all elements of a webpage to be fully displayed.

Local marketing - There are two types of local marketing. If you are a local business, you will focus your marketing on your immediate location. You wouldn't spend resources getting your brand in front of audiences that are nowhere near you, geographically. The other type is when you customize your marketing based on where it will be seen, geographically. An ecommerce site, for example, may customize the products they market based on the interests or seasons of particular regions instead of showing the exact same content everywhere.

Long tail keywords - These are longer variations on your primary keywords or phrases that people are likely to use when they're closer to purchase, or deep in their research phase. For example, "SEO resources" would be a primary keyword, whereas "resource book the SEO way buy online" is a long tail keyword. These keywords have relatively low search volume, but typically have a much higher conversion rate.

Macro conversion - Any conversion that your business deems most important. See "Conversion" above.

Marketing strategy - A business's overall approach to marketing its products or services.

Measurement - The practice of measuring the results of campaigns or the performance of a web property.

Medium - The singular of "media". In marketing, a medium is typically a single source. For example, all social networks fall under the umbrella of "social media", but one specific network, such as Facebook or LinkedIn, would be considered a social medium.

Messaging - The words you use to talk about and promote your brand or business. A best practice for building solid brand awareness is to establish a clear, compelling message and to be consistent in using only that messaging.

Meta data - The data about your data. Examples include page titles, file names, image titles, etc.

Meta description - This is the little description of the page that shows up under the meta title on search engine results pages. Its primary purpose is to entice users to click. By increasing your click through rate, the meta description helps to indirectly increase your SEO strength as search engines prioritize user behaviour metrics like click through rate. See also "Meta title".

Meta keywords - A type of meta tag used to indicate what the webpage is about. These tags no longer hold as much SEO weight as they once did as they were, in the past, improperly used to try to game the system through keyword stuffing. However, they still hold a small amount of weight in SEO and are worth your attention. Today, common uses of these tags are to include misspellings of your main keywords, the plural versions of your keywords and your long tail keywords to tell search engines that your content is relevant to those variations. See also "Keyword stuffing" and "Long tail keywords".

Meta title - This is the title of a page that appears at the very top of your browser (or as the title of the browser tab) and as the title in search engine results pages.

Mobile - Mobile devices such as tablets or smartphones.

Mobile site - The version of your website that is adapted for mobile devices.

Multivariate test - A test of multiple elements within a webpage. Multivariate tests can be incredibly granular and incredibly insightful. For example, you may test the elements of a single button: button text, button colour, font, rounded corners vs. square, etc.

Natural links - Links from one domain/site to another that occur organically, rather than through paid content or ads. For example, if a blog reviews your product with no incentive from you and links to your website without using any tracking code on the link, that would be a natural link. Natural links have no tracking code, are not embedded in ads and don't pass through any kind of monetization software.

No-follow link - A "nofollow" attribute can be added to certain links or to full pages, telling search engines to, essentially, not follow those links. Links from one site to another are a signal to search engines that the linked-to site is valuable in some way, and helps that site build SEO strength. So, why use "nofollow"? A common use is for comment sections. If you use an automatic nofollow attribute for all comments on your blog or product pages, it prevents spam. Have you ever seen those comments that have absolutely nothing to do with the page content and link to some product or service? Those are spammy attempts at building the SEO strength of the linked-to page or site. Implementing nofollow for all comments will prevent this, as these spammers are unlikely to waste their time where there's no value to them.

Off-page SEO - The aspects of your SEO strategy that occur outside your page or site. Link building is one example, as is social media marketing, as the link referrals are occurring off-site. See also "Link building" and "Social media marketing".

On-page SEO - The aspects of your SEO strategy that occur within your website. Examples include content creation, meta data, site structure, speedy load times and keyword mapping.

Optimization - The practice of using every resource and insight available to you to improve your web properties, marketing strategies, etc. in order to increase business success.

Open graph tags - These tags allow you to control the description that is shown when your site or page is shared on Facebook. See also "Twitter card tags".

Organic search - Also called natural search. When a search engine user types in a search term, the non-paid generated results are considered organic search. They are the result of search engine spiders crawling the web to gather data and the search engine algorithms determining which results best match the user's search terms and other demographic information. See "Paid search" below.

Page extension - The part of a URL that comes after the main domain name. For example, www.google.com would be a main domain name. In the case of www.google.com/maps, the /maps part of the URL is called the page extension.

Page rank - Also written as PageRank. It is a Google algorithm used to determine how webpages will rank on their results pages. Although the name seems obvious - it's for ranking pages, so it's called PageRank - it is actually named for Google cofounder, Larry Page. See also "Rank".

Paid search - The practice of paying to have your business's ad appear on search engine results pages when users search for certain keywords or phrases.

Persona - A profile of your target audience. In marketing, it can help in creating truly engaging and authentic content to imagine creating it for a specific individual. This can also help you in targeting that content effectively. Typically, you would want to have several personas, depending on the demographics of your typical customer(s) or target customer(s).

PHP - Also called Hypertext Preprocessor. In its early days, it was called Personal Home Page, which is where the PHP acronym comes from. It is a server-side coding language, meaning it deals with server functions. HTML, on the other hand, is a front-end language that deals with the visual elements displayed to the user, whereas PHP works on the backend/server-side to populate the content your HTML works to display.

Query - A query is essentially a question to be answered. When a search engine user types in their search terms, that is one example of a query. When you create a report in GA with filters, that is also a query.

Rank - In marketing, rank typically refers to where your business's listing shows up in organic search results for particular keywords or phrases. For example, if you are a Montreal-based bicycle store and your listing shows up in fourth place when someone searches for "Montreal bike shops", you have a ranking of 4. See "Organic search" above.

Real time - In this exact moment. For example, when you view the real time report in GA, you are seeing the activity taking place on your web property at this exact moment.

Redirect test - This is when you want to compare the performance of different landing pages. An example of a redirect test may be to send an email newsletter to your full subscriber list with a link to "shop now". Your list would be randomly split in two and clicking the "shop now" link would redirect them to either the specific product page or to the product department page to see which one performs best in generating sales.

Remarketing - The practice of targeting ads to people who have visited your web property but did not make a purchase or otherwise convert (See "Conversion" above). If you have ever visited a website and left without purchasing, then started seeing ads for that site pop up in your social networks and search listings, that's remarketing.

Return on investment (ROI) - The monetary return generated from investing in a marketing campaign or other effort to increase sales. Obviously, you want your return to be greater than what you put in. Ideally much greater.

Robots.txt - A text file that guides search engine bots on how to crawl the pages on your website. See also "Bots".

Search engine - A web service used to search for products, services or other information on the web. Examples include Google, Bing and Yahoo.

Search engine marketing (SEM) - The practice of increasing your website's visibility in search engine results. Typically, this is done by paying for ad listings. See "Paid search" above.

Search engine optimization (SEO) - The practice of optimizing your website structure, content and linking (See "Link building" above) in order to increase your website's visibility in organic search results (See "Organic search" above).

Search engine results page (SERP) - The page of results shown after a search engine user types in their search query.

Search performance - The performance of your web property in organic search results. See "Organic search" and "Rank" above.

Search ranking - The ranking of your web property in organic search results. See "Organic search", "Rank" and "Page rank" above.

Search term - The terms entered into a search engine by a user in order to find specific products, services or other information.

Seasonal trends - From an SEO perspective, this usually refers to keywords and long tail keywords that users use on a seasonal basis. "Winter tires" would be an example of a seasonal trend, as there is typically a seasonal spike in searches for that keyword. See also "Keywords" and "Long tail keywords".

Site search - Search capabilities embedded within a website. Whenever you visit a website and are able to search within that site using an embedded search tool, that's site search.

Site speed - The speed with which a site loads pages and page elements.

Site structure - Refers to how the pages within your site are linked together both visually and in the background. This matters from a user experience perspective (how easily people are able to find things and navigate your site) and an SEO perspective (how easily search engines are able to find the content on your site). This is especially important for websites that have many pages such as ecommerce sites or online magazines.

Sitelink - These are the links that sometimes appear under a search result in a search engine results page (See "Search engine results page" above). They typically link to subpages within the main website.

Sitemap XML - A file produced and maintained solely for search engines. It is one of the few instances where your SEO will put the search engine first, rather than the user. This file lists all your site URLs (i.e. the URLs for every individual page) in plain text, making it easy for search engines to navigate your site. With large sites that have many pages, there are different strategies for ensuring a well-structured sitemap.

Social media - Any platform or tool through which users are able to engage, socially, with each other. For example, Facebook, LinkedIn, Twitter and Instagram are all examples of social media, but a comments section or forum may also be considered a form of social media.

Social media marketing - Any type of marketing carried out through social media. Maintaining a Facebook business page, for example, is a form of social media marketing.

SSL certificate - Stands for Secure Sockets Layer. It is a digital certificate that indicates a secure connection, ensuring any data passed between the user's browser and the website remains private and secure. Originally intended to secure online credit card transactions, it is also used to secure login information, data transfers, and is now becoming a standard security measure across all sites. An SSL certificate is usually indicated by a little padlock icon in your browser's address bar.

Staging environment - A server where the environment is set to look and function exactly like the production environment (i.e. the actual website or application). Its purpose is to verify that a new fix, feature or version is fully functional and ready to be delivered to users. See also "Development environment".

Tags - A tag is a form of meta data (See "Meta data" above). It is information about information. For example, when you tag someone in a picture on Facebook, you are providing information (a person's identity) about information (the picture). From a software perspective, a tag is used to provide information about the information within site code.

Target market - The set of demographic data you want to target in your marketing efforts is your target market. For example, you may be targeting millennials of a particular income bracket living in a certain geographical area. A target market can also be campaign based. For example, an ecommerce site like Amazon sells a range of products that cater to just about anyone on Earth. Instead of marketing to the entire world, they create specific target markets to market to (See also "Persona" above).

Tracking code - The snippets of code used to track pages, links or entire websites for analytics purposes.

Traditional marketing - Marketing that takes place outside the digital realm. Television commercials (even though most TVs are digital today, commercials existed pre-digital), magazine advertorials, direct mailings, etc. are all examples of traditional marketing.

Traffic - The flow of visitors to your website or web property.

Traffic sources - Where your visitors come from. They may be coming from search engines, social media, blogs, online articles, email newsletters, etc.

Trend - A pattern. From a digital marketing perspective, we examine data to identify trends or patterns in things like visits, sales, clicks, etc. in order to capitalize on them.

Trend measurement - The practice of measuring trends in the market. Twitter card tags - Similar to open graph tags, but for Twitter, these allow you to control how your content is displayed when your webpage is shared on Twitter. See also "Open graph tags" above.

URL - The web address of a site or page. https://thecaminowith.com is an example of a URL. https://thecaminowithin.com/buy-camino-within/, although within the same site, is a unique URL.

URL parameters - This is a tag added to a URL either for tracking purposes or to send users to a specific landing page, such as a product page. These parameters always come after a question mark and use an equal sign and ampersand, so it would look something like this: www.example.com?pagetype=abc&utm_source=google.

User driven metrics - Metrics based on user behaviour. Examples of user driven metrics include average time on site, bounce rate, pages per visit, etc.

User experience - The experience a visitor has when interacting with your site or web property. This includes load time, site structure, general functionality, level of engagement with content, etc. (See "Content", "Engagement", "Load time" and "Site structure" above).

User flow - The steps a user must take to complete a conversion or other goal.

UTM tag - Urchin Tracking Module. A UTM tag is a snippet of code added to the end of a URL for tracking purposes. This allows you to track specific campaigns (specific newsletters or ads, for example) or traffic sources (social networks or blog posts, for example).

Visitors - The people visiting your site or web property.

Web property - A web-based property for which you (or your company) are the owner. This may be a website, a mobile app, a community forum, etc., but it must be solely owned by you (or your business). A social network profile like LinkedIn, for example, is technically owned by the social network, therefore, it would not be considered a property.

White hat - This is the gold standard in SEO approaches. White hat strategies and tactics follow search engine rules and regulations, as well as general SEO best practices to build solid SEO strength. It also keeps the user experience front of mind. See "Black hat" above.

Word of mouth - A form of marketing and/or lead and sales acquisition that relies on users or customers telling their friends, family, colleagues, etc. about your business, product or service.

Acronyms to remember

GA = Google Analytics
SEO = Search Engine Optimization
SEM = Search Engine Marketing (also known as paid search)
GTM = Google Tag Manager
HTTP = Hyper Text Transfer Protocol
HTTPs = Hyper Text Transfer Protocol Secure
CMS = Content Management System
CRO = Conversion Rate Optimization
CTA = Call to Action
LSEO = Local Search Engine Optimization
ROI = Return on Investment
SE = Search Engine
SERP = Search Engine Results Page
URL = Uniform Resource Locator
UX = User Experience
LPO = Landing Page Optimization
HTML = Hypertext Markup Language

Chapter 1

What is SEO?

>>>

What is Search Engine Optimization?

SEO is an acronym for Search Engine Optimization. It is the practice of optimizing your site or web property to meet search engine guidelines and rules.

Why does this matter? In a way, search engines rule the internet. When someone is searching for a specific product or service, looking for help or solutions, seeking out new ideas... they use search engines! And it's the search engines that determine what results people will see when they enter certain search terms. To do this, search engines design their own sets of rules and regulations known as algorithms. As the engines crawl virtually everything on the web, the algorithms get busy categorizing, filtering and, ultimately, ranking everything they find to determine how and where (and even if!) each result will show up on search results pages.

That's a lot of influence.

Over the years, SEO strategies have evolved. The way consumers search has also evolved. As a result, search engines have also had to evolve and the algorithms they design have been getting smarter and smarter. Ultimately, search engines want people to find what they're looking for. If they couldn't, they'd stop using the search engines. Because of this, algorithms have evolved to heavily favor the user, meaning SEO also must favor the user if it is going to be successful.

3 SEO Truths

- SEO Truth #1: The only constant is change. Google used to update their algorithms 5 to 10 times a year. Now they update their algorithms a few times everyday.

- SEO Truth #2: There is no silver bullet and there never will be. You will never be able to find that one solution that works over and over again. When it comes to designing a successful SEO strategy, the ideal approach is one of "leave no stone unturned" as opposed to "find the silver bullet".

- SEO Truth #3: There are no guarantees. If it ever happens that someone guarantees a particular SEO result, consider that your cue to walk away.

Chapter 1.1

Digital Marketing

I once used the good ol' Yellow Pages as a means of explaining digital marketing and online search to someone whose age made them more familiar with phone booths than social media. It turned out to be a helpful analogy but, the reality is, there's a lot more to digital marketing than search. Digital marketing is an ever-evolving mix of different digital channels that you can use to promote and drive value to your business. And, while SEO is one part of digital marketing, almost all other digital marketing channels have the power to impact your SEO.

- -

Digital marketing channels:

- SEO (Search Engine Optimization): The process of aligning the various elements of your site (tags, content, data, information, links, etc.) with the best practices of search engines, so that you can rank as high as possible in search engine results.
- SEM (Search Engine Marketing): The process of implementing search and display campaigns on advertising platforms such as Google Ads and Bing Ads, with the aim of creating relevant traffic and awareness for your brand and website.
- Social Media Marketing: The process of marketing your brand and website on social channels to create awareness, loyalty, retention, traffic and conversions.
  - o Most common social channels: Facebook, Twitter, LinkedIn, Instagram, etc.
- Email Marketing: The process of collecting email subscribers, then creating and sending email campaigns intended to grow brand awareness and sell more products and services, or otherwise convert subscribers such as encouraging event sign ups, content downloads, etc.
  - o Common email marketing platforms: Mailchimp, Constant Contact, GetResponse, SendinBlue (this is a highly saturated market, and there are many to choose from)

- Content Marketing: The process of creating and sharing videos, articles, images and other forms of digital content.
- Local Marketing: The process of marketing your product or service to specific geographical locations or neighborhoods.
- Landing Page Marketing: The process of creating highly targeted landing pages and directing traffic to said pages based on a set of predetermined criteria. The main goal of these pages is to get visitors to stay longer on your site and convert (buy, signup, etc.)
    - Landing page marketing is also known as CRO or Conversion Rate Optimization.

We just covered the main types of digital marketing, but there are many more, with new techniques and tools evolving regularly.

For the sake of brevity, and in the interest of giving you the most 'bang for your buck', the marketing types listed above cover the bulk of what digital marketing is today.

It is important to know that these channels of digital marketing work best together. Alone, they will not yield great results. Combined, they become incredibly powerful.

For example, many people look at SEO as some kind of magic bullet. They'll say to me, "Tarek, I want to work on my site SEO. I want it to rank number 1, organically."

My answer is always as follows:

1. There are no guarantees in SEO so that I won't promise you. What I can promise is to leave no stone unturned; no digital channel untapped.
2. SEO doesn't work on its own. Let's talk about your business and see how your other channels are working, or not working.
3. Let's talk about how your business can benefit the most from many different channels, instead of just one.

In short, don't expect to put all your eggs in one basket.

Takeaway

Digital marketing is a consistent, logical strategy of which SEO is one element. It's not, "Let's try this now and that later." For digital marketing to drive results, it must be holistic and consistent.

What role does SEO play in digital marketing?

To go back to the Yellow Pages analogy, SEO is the strategy that gets your web properties listed and seen. Whereas people once searched alphabetically, "the Yellow Pages of today" (i.e. search engines) focuses on the intent of the user and giving them the best possible results based on a number of keywords, location, demographic and other factors. So, you can have the best content marketing strategy the world has ever seen, but if you don't factor in SEO, your target audience may never see that content.

Exercise

Create a diagram like the one in this chapter. Highlight the channels you are currently tapping into and which ones you need to start working on.
This will help you get a clear 360° view of what can be improved, what opportunities are being missed, and where you're doing well (remember that marketing is as much about celebrating the wins as it is about learning from setbacks).

Draw your business diagram here:

Chapter 2

Things You Need to Know About Digital Marketing

>>

Things You Need to Know

As entrepreneurs and business owners, we're always looking to take our businesses to the next level. Inevitably, digital marketing will come up as an avenue to evaluate. Despite being an avenue teeming with potential and opportunity, many entrepreneurs hesitate. **As a marketer, these are the reasons I hear over and over again:**

"It's just not the right time."
"My product isn't where I want it to be yet, so it's too early."
"I don't think it's the best ROI for me."
"I don't have the budget for digital right now."
"I just don't feel that digital is the way to go."
"My product does not need digital marketing."

My advice is this: If you haven't started yet, stop finding reasons not to and invest in digital marketing now.

Digital marketing is like vitamins for your business -- essential to growth. To compete and grow your presence, you need your vitamins.

Here are four things you need to understand about the importance of running digital marketing in parallel with product and service development:

- -

1. Digital marketing doesn't have to cost an arm and a leg

One of the biggest benefits of digital marketing is flexibility. That flexibility extends to cost as well.

Successful digital marketing starts by creating authentic, unique and relevant content, which can be as simple and inexpensive as putting pen to paper (or fingers to keyboard).

Start with the question, "What keeps my target client up at night?" From there, start writing blog posts that address the questions and concerns they might have.

These kinds of posts boost search performance. As people search for answers to their questions, your website will show up. Depending on the blogging platform you use, these posts are also free, or very low cost. As we'll discuss in later chapters, good content creation can be one of the most impactful AND inexpensive elements of a solid SEO strategy.

Once you have your awesome content, ensure it's listed, categorized and optimized properly.

What does this mean? Use relevant tags for each post. For example, if you're selling pet products, use "pet products" as a tag. If the post is specifically about dog beds, use "pet products," "dog beds" and maybe "dog sleep solutions." Get it? Your blogging platform probably has a simple field for tags that you have to fill in.

Optimize your post by ensuring the title, headlines and content are aligned and reinforce the keywords you think people will most likely use in their searches. Consider a title like, "Top 5 Dog Beds for Canine Insomnia". You score "dog beds" and "canine insomnia" as keywords.

- -

2. Digital marketing is as much about the buildup as it is about the kickoff

Building up to a product launch is as important as the launch itself. Most successful marketers know how to introduce the right teasers, trailers and previews at the right time to get the hype up for a product or service release.

Take the movie industry, for example. Before a movie hits the theatre, you'll see at least one teaser, a few trailers and plenty of content spread across a certain time period. The build-up is sometimes even more intense than the movie!

How does this translate to entrepreneurs in other industries? You're probably not going to create Hollywood-esque trailers. Instead, cultivate a certain following on social media by sharing teasers about your upcoming product. Build traction using images and video on multiple channels. Use the power of social media to create excitement around your brand or concept and how it will change people's lives for the better.

Use teasers like, "The ultimate solution to conquering bathroom tile mould is just three days away!" Make it exciting. Make it intriguing. Throw some humour in if you can. Don't give it all away. Just get people interested. All of this will ultimately feed into your SEO as well.

3. Every product or service, no matter how good, needs digital marketing

The stats are staggering. According to recent statistics by Hootsuite & Internet World Stats, there are now more than 4 billion internet users worldwide. It's a playing field that can't be ignored. Seeing as most people are on the web and we're spending more and more time surfing on our phones than ever before, it simply makes no sense to overlook digital marketing.

No matter your ideal target, statistically speaking it's highly likely they are on the web, meaning opportunities exist to target them directly and effectively, and how you rank in search engines DOES matter. Connect with people with the right content, at the right time, with the right message and you will reach a much bigger audience with much less investment than with almost any other marketing outlet. How do you know the right content and time? We'll be getting to that further along in this book.

4. You don't have to hire ten different agencies to run your digital marketing

You can start doing all of the above on your own.

When you're ready to invest a bit more, hire just one agency that will work with you to integrate SEO and content marketing. Many entrepreneurs hire two different agencies, but a good agency will do both.

When you marry your search strategy with your content strategy, it will yield a higher ROI for your business and, logistically, it's much easier to work with just one agency.

Takeaway

All entrepreneurs and small business owners should venture into digital marketing and should not wait for the 'ideal moment.' Nothing is ever perfect. It's about making the best of where you are now and moving forward.

The 'ideal moment' is now. It's always now. If you don't start now, someone else in your space will.

Exercise

Write down your business goals for this year. If you're currently a student, think up a fictional business or imagine you're already working for (or running) your dream company, and consider what the goals of that business might be.

The most effective marketing of any kind, digital or otherwise, is aligned with the goals of the business. When you are clear on your business goals, you can read this book with them in mind, and are open to the possibilities and opportunities that exist for you. This will help you understand how SEO and digital marketing will help you reach your goals.

Chapter 3

Way of Thinking

Before marketing became all about numbers, rankings, data, optimizations, trends and improvements... it was something else. It was a way of thinking. So, before we continue on, let's explore the success way of thinking when it comes to marketing.

Think Value and Authenticity

The most successful marketing brings value and authenticity. Successful analytics is about deriving the insight and intelligence to know how best to bring value and show authenticity.

In a world where everyone is trying to speak louder than everyone else, it is value and your authentic brand that will speak loudest for you.

As you create campaigns and design strategies, think about the emotions or motivations of your target audience. It's not unlike car ads. Sexy, sleek cars with beautiful, scantily clad women highlight a certain motivation beyond smart design or fuel efficiency. Rugged 4x4's with young, fit millennials sell adventure, not advanced safety features. And minivans smartly loaded with camping or sporting equipment, complete with four smiling kids piling out sell family values. Identify the values of your audience, then build honest, authentic content that reflects the values you're bringing forward.

Providing value builds a relationship of mutual respect with your audience and a sense of camaraderie; a sense of "we understand and we're in this with you.".

Of course, profit is important. You're running a business after all. But making money cannot be the starting point of your marketing. The money may be your goal, but it isn't your audience's. When profit takes second place to delivering value, you connect with your audience more authentically, and profit will follow.

It is through giving that we become better as humans, and it is through delivering value that we become better as businesses.*

*If you're wondering what this has to do with SEO and search rankings, don't worry. We're building foundations right now - critical foundations. Keep reading and the full structure will emerge.

Teach something. Use the educational approach.

When a consumer has questions, they want to be helped, not sold to. And they are acutely aware of the difference.

They want to be educated, not pushed. Advised, not harassed. They will instinctively ignore an onslaught of advertising but engage with content that brings them value.

"But wait, I need to sell. That's how I keep the lights on!"

Of course, but remember that you're far more likely to make a sale if you give the customer what they want. And they are far more likely to talk to other people about it. Give them a good experience!

Be the face in the crowd that is educating and delivering real value. Provide tips, news and ideas relevant to your brand, product and target market. What are your client's pain points? What are they stressing about? Create content that addresses these issues.

When you are seen as a source of knowledge, you are seen as an expert. When they feel that pain, they will also feel that you understand it and can help with it.

And all that great, educational content? Search engines love it too. By putting education first, you're putting that all-important value first, and that pays off for your business in numerous ways.

Think Mobile

The thing about mobile devices like smartphones and tablets is that they're... well... mobile. That's why most mobile search results are location based.

Search for restaurant recommendations while you're at the office, for example, and you'll get results for restaurants in the immediate area. And when someone is looking for a good lunch spot while on the go, they're not going to go home to check their computer. They're going to whip out their phone.

That's why a responsive, easy to navigate and mobile-friendly site is an absolute must.

As a bonus, Google factors mobile-friendliness into their search rankings, so a mobile-friendly site can also improve your overall search rankings.
Not sure if your site is mobile friendly? Thankfully, there's a tool for that.
Isn't the future great? Check if your site is mobile friendly
here: **https://www.google.com/webmasters/tools/mobile-friendly**.

Think Speed

Fact: Site speed and performance are becoming more and more important. There are many reasons for that, but the most important are:

1. Making visitors wait even 4-10 seconds for a page to load will likely lead to a lost conversion.
2. All search engines consider site-speed as a ranking signal.
3. No one wants to wait.
4. Our attention span is getting shorter.
5. We want everything now.

We're in an age of same day delivery. We binge watch instead of waiting for new episodes. We get our news when we want it instead of waiting for the next broadcast. Some industries - like the food industry and the slow food movement - are benefiting from a 'back to the old days' nostalgia. The internet will not be one of them. If you want to compete, you have to be fast.

Don't Always Think Budget

A low budget is not an issue. Inaction is an issue. The most important thing is to start somewhere and measure results. Even a small investment will give you something to analyze and optimize, so that you can continue to improve results and drive more business. All you need is that first seed, and you can grow from there.

For local businesses to thrive, digital marketing is a must. Searching online is now the number one method people use to find the products, services and businesses they're looking for. You need to make sure they're finding you, and they're getting the best possible experience when they do.

Concentrate on intent, not just keywords.

As we move more and more towards voice search, mobile-first indexing, and machine learning algorithms, search and SEO are becoming more and more... intentional.

At least in the sense that you must focus on the intentions of your market. If the content you generate and share is going to successfully build strong SEO, it cannot be based solely on keywords. The intent of your audience must also be taken into account.

What do I mean by this?

Intention, in search, is about the meaning behind a search query and not simply the words used.

Let's say you are looking for a gym and type "gym" into Google. Go ahead. Give it a try.

Notice that Google doesn't give the definition of the word "gym". It doesn't give you the history of gyms, or even an alphabetical list of gyms.

No. Google anticipates your intention. It assumes you are looking for a gym in your neighborhood. The first results you see will be the Google local listings for gyms near you, then a list of search results for gyms in your area and gym directories, typically listed based on an algorithm of user reviews, link popularity and many other factors.

Google's mission is, "To organize the world's information and make it universally accessible and useful."

For me, the most important part of Google's mission statement is the last two words: accessible and useful.

We are constantly moving to more relevant and smarter search results - results that are more and more accessible and useful. Relevancy, accessibility and usefulness depend heavily on understanding the intent of the audience, then planning your content and other marketing strategies around that intent.

Later on in this book, we'll look at a few measurement tools like Google Analytics and Google Trends. When we do, keep in mind that we have to think beyond the simple terms and clicks, and concentrate on what the users have in mind; on being accessible and useful.

Think Local in Your Messaging

Your messaging - the words, phrases and sentences you use on your site - has a big impact on your search results. Be sure to work your location into your messaging.

For example, if you are a Montreal-based photographer specializing in headshots, use phrases like "Montreal headshots," "Montreal headshot photographer" and "headshot photography Montreal." More generic phrases, like "headshot photographer," are too broad, difficult to rank for and don't capitalize on your location.

Think local in your messaging and you'll not only get much more relevant results, you'll also save time and money by not trying to rank for those broad, highly competitive terms.

Think First Impressions

For most businesses, brick and mortar storefronts are no longer a customer's first impression. People today go online to find virtually everything. Your website is now your first impression. And just as in real life, first impressions are everything on the internet.

Be ready for your customer's arrival. Just as you would keep a physical store looking its best, make sure your website is up to date, well structured, gives off the right impression and highlights your most important information.

That may be your mission statement, a call to action, instructions for how to contact you, a login form - whatever is most important for your customers to see first and foremost.

Think Engagement

Although "SEO" stands for Search Engine Optimization, the optimization you do is truly more for humans than search engines. After all, people are your customers. Not the engines.

To rank well, think about the human experience rather than the search engines. **Focus on human engagement**, relevancy to searchers, and what will be most attractive to the people, rather than stuffing in keywords just to appeal to search engines.

Search engines do respond to a well-structured site with solid keyword and linking strategies. However, they also give weight to how visitors interact with your site - how often they click, how long they spend on your site, the number of pages they visit, etc. They also consider the types of sites linking to yours, and you are far more likely to have reputable blogs, businesses, e-magazines and even social media users linking to your content if it is engaging and delivers value. Those technical elements and other strategies targeting the search engines alone quickly lose their value in the "eyes" of search engines if real humans aren't showing interest.

Create for people and the search engines will follow.

Think Build Up

Many consumers look into new products or services before they are even released. Based on a Google study, for example, moviegoers typically start looking into new movies a month before their release date.

The same is often true for product releases. Many consumers love a good product buildup. They read reviews, speculative blogs, watch videos and interviews, sign up for email updates, enter contests, and sometimes even pre-order so they can be among the very first to get the latest new thing. In your digital marketing efforts, this is a huge opportunity to build hype, brand awareness and engagement.

Probably the most well-known company to do this for products is Apple. Historically, they've done this really well and you can certainly look to them for ideas and inspiration. Just don't use Apple as your benchmark. They're a huge company with a massive following, and very few companies can match them. Instead, keep your focus on your target market. Where are they? What are they reading or watching? What are they searching for? What gets them fired up? Use that to create an engaging pre-release campaign that delivers value.

Capitalize on your pre-release period and you can carry that hype through into post-release. You don't need to be huge. You do need to be engaging.

Understand That There is No One-Size-Fits-All Approach

What you want to achieve and when you want to achieve it will differ from other businesses in your market. Your messaging will be different. Your creative will be different. Your corporate culture, quarterly objectives, and staff resources will all be different.

What works for one business won't necessarily be the right fit for your business. Approach all your marketing, including SEO and search marketing, in a way that makes sense for your business - its values, culture, objectives, mission and resources.

For example, building organic SEO establishes long term visibility, typically with higher conversions. But, it takes commitment and time before you see results. SEM (search engine marketing), on the other hand, delivers results only for your period of investment, but the results are more immediate.

What do you want to achieve? What are your resources? When do you want or need to see results? Understand this first before making any investment of time or resources.

Takeaway

Give before taking.
Intentions before keywords.
First impressions matter.

Exercise

Create a checklist like the one below to see where your thinking is aligned when it comes to your business and where it could be improved.
Ask yourself, "Is my business mindset aligned with a successful digital marketing mindset?" Remember, SEO is holistic. All areas of your digital marketing strategy will influence SEO success, either directly or indirectly.

What do you want to achieve?

What are your resources?

When do you want or need to see results?

MINDSET	MY BUSINESS MINDSET
THINK VALUE	
THINK EDUCATION	
THINK MOBILE	
THINK SPEED	
DON'T ALWAYS THINK BUDGET	
THINK INTENTION	
THINK LOCAL IN YOUR MESSAGING	
THINK FIRST IMPRESSION	
THINK ENGAGEMENT	
THINK BUILD UP	
THINK TAILORED APPROACH	

Chapter 4

SEO and the Consumer Journey

>>>>>>>>>>>>>>>>>>>>>>>>>>>>>>>>>>>>>>>

To be successful, SEO must consider the consumer journey. This is incredibly important.

We can't approach SEO with a one-dimensional strategy or viewpoint. we need to make sure that we are optimizing our site with terms that match each part of the journey.

A typical journey includes awareness, consideration and purchase. The terms a person enters into a search engine will reflect their stage in that journey. As such, you will want to optimize your site for terms that cater to each of the three stages.

Awareness

Consideration

Purchase

What does this look like in practice? Let's use my first book as an example. It's called "The Camino Within" and it is a motivational and inspirational book recounting my experiences along the famed pilgrimage, the Camino de Santiago (in my personal, and obviously biased opinion, a pretty great book!).

Let's imagine we are optimizing the website for "The Camino Within". What terms might we optimize for to address the awareness, consideration and purchase stages of the consumer journey?

Awareness terms will be: "Motivational Book", "Self Help Book", "Personal Growth book".

At this stage, the consumer has identified their particular need or want. Through searching those terms, we hope they become aware of our book and it's potential to fulfill their quest.

Consideration terms will be: "Camino De Santiago book", "Books on Pilgrims".

At this stage, the consumer is evaluating how well our book may suit their needs, including how it might compare to others of a similar topic. We want to ensure to rank for these terms so that our book continues to show up as the consumer conducts their research.

Purchase terms will be: "The Camino Within", "Where to buy the Camino within?"

The consumer is ready to buy. Hooray! We need to ensure they can easily find where to get it and complete their purchase. We can't assume they're still on our site and staring at a big "buy now" button. If they've moved on to something else, then come back to buy, there's a good chance their first stop will be Google.

SEO and Company Goals

>>>

As mentioned in the beginning of this book, SEO is but one player in the digital marketing game, as opposed to the only player.

That being said, it is part of a bigger company and marketing strategy. Remember that SEO works best when the company is working and when marketing is working.

As you set up your marketing strategy, always bear in mind what the company goals are. Likewise, as you set up your SEO strategy, make sure it is aligned with the marketing strategy of the company (which is aligned with the company goals... align, align, align!).

SEO
Strategy

Marketing
Strategy

Company's Goals

Takeaway

SEO is but one player in your overall digital marketing and business strategies. Like any good team, your players need to be aligned to be successful. So, when it comes to SEO, take your other players into account - players like the consumer journey and company goals. Get them working together, supporting each other, working towards the same outcome. That's how you cross the finish line.

Chapter 5

White Hat vs Black Hat SEO

>>

The Good vs Evil of SEO

If you're a fan of Game of Thrones, then you understand that there is rarely a clear divide between good and evil. Similarly (though less bloody), there is a lot of grey area when it comes to SEO tactics. And, if we go back to the first truth of SEO, remember that change is the only constant. What was ok ten years ago, is not ok now.

There is no clear code of everything that's right and everything that's wrong, and what we understand as a best practice vs. a terrible or murky practice today, will change.

Yet, there are some things that we can all agree are fundamentally bad, and things that we can all agree are fundamentally good.

This is what white vs. black hat SEO is all about.

White Hat SEO

In a nutshell, White hat SEO is good SEO; the SEO that you should be doing to make sure that your site is up there on the search engine results. White hat SEO techniques include:

- Optimizing for users, not search engines
- Bringing value to your site visitors by addressing their search queries
- Creating relevant content on your site
- Using terms and keywords moderately
- Avoiding plagiarism and being original

Black Hat SEO

Black hat SEO tactics include:
- Keyword stuffing
- Optimizing for search engines instead of humans
- Getting shady backlinks to the site
- Using click bait
- Buying traffic
- Using confusing terms
- Cloaking

From an SEO and business perspective, these are considered just straight up bad ideas, if not unethical. The thing is, they also won't work long term. A bunch of shady backlinks, or stuffing your content full of keywords that make the content practically unreadable, may generate an initial boost in your search rankings and burst of traffic. However, it won't last and the search engines aren't going to like it when they realize what you're doing. Remember earlier in the book when I noted that search engine algorithms are getting smarter and smarter? They're not just getting better at catering to users. They're also getting really good at filtering out sites that use black hat tactics.

Finally, if you're bringing in visitors by essentially tricking them, are these really the types of visitors that are going to convert to paying customers? Unlikely.

Everything you will learn in this book is considered white hat SEO. As much as black hat might bring results in the moment, it is truly not sustainable in the long run, and could potentially damage your site's reputation with search engines.

Practice safe search. Use your white hat.

Takeaway

Focus on the long game. Black hat tactics can be tempting because they sometimes bring fast results in terms of rankings. However, those rankings rarely lead to a significant boost in conversions, and the tactics you use can get you penalized by search engines. That's hard to come back from. White hat tactics take longer to see results, but the results are lasting and more likely to drive conversions. Remember the alignment lessons from the previous chapter and remember to prioritize the user experience. Users appreciate it, search engines appreciate it and your business will appreciate it.

Chapter 6

Ranking Factors

>>

The Evolution of Search Marketing

Long ago, before I can remember, search engines used to trust those of us who worked as search engine experts. But, as all good stories go, betrayal was afoot! Time and time again, we search engine experts continued to trick the algorithm in different ways to get the best rankings possible. We worked to game the system instead of providing real value.

The search engines became unhappy.

So, as time passed, search engines became more secretive about their algorithm updates and started taking control out of the hands of SEO experts.

By 2018-2019, search engine ranking factors were no longer impacted by the direct changes we experts were making on-site. Instead, the user became king and user metrics became the ultimate drivers of search engine rankings. Quite the saga! That story helps us understand where we are today in terms of SEO, and what we need to do to be successful.

The online visibility management service, SEMrush, recently conducted a study that showed that in the past 2 years, time on site, pages per session, bounce rate and number of visits have become the most important ranking factors for a web property. And, as time moves on, search engines are extremely likely to continue that trend of focusing on the user over the experts, which means we experts need to focus on the user as well.

What does that tell us as SEO experts?

- Optimize with users in mind!
  - o We must ensure that we are creating good, original, engaging content that delivers real value and keeps visitors on our sites longer.
  - o We should not rely solely on SEO to bring traffic, but all other sources of traffic to do so as well.
  - o We should create a diversity of content that will keep users engaged.
  - o We should make our content more readable/watchable/consumable.
  - o We should understand the user flow on our site and optimize for it.

Takeaway

Optimize with the user in mind! The whole reason search engines exist is to help people find what they're looking for on the internet. It makes sense that, as much as possible, search engines will prioritize the user in determining search rankings. If you do the same, search engines will prioritize you.

Chapter 7

Search Intent

More Than Just Keywords

As we are moving more and more towards voice search, mobile-first indexing, and machine learning algorithms, search and SEO are becoming more and more... intentional.

At least in the sense that you must focus on the intentions of your market.

If the content is to successfully build strong SEO, it cannot be based solely on keywords. The INTENT of your audience must also be taken into account.

What do I mean by this?

As mentioned earlier in this book "intention" is the meaning behind a search query and not simply the words used.

Last time, we used the gym example. This time, let's consider your favourite band. If you type just the band name into Google, the first result will probably be the band's official website. But look at all the other results. Google is trying to figure out your intent in searching the band name. It's most likely also showing you YouTube results, a tour schedule, and where to buy tickets for the next show in, or closest to, your city. Even when you typed in the name, Google probably also suggested more targeted searches by adding on "albums", "concerts", etc.

And whatever you click or navigate to after entering your search, Google will use that to learn about you and users in general so that they can continually improve their algorithm and search results going forward.

As we reviewed earlier, **Google's mission is "To organize the world's information and make it universally accessible and useful."**

And what were the two most important words of that statement? Accessible and useful!

We are constantly moving to more relevant and smarter search results – results that are more and more accessible and useful. Relevancy, accessibility and usefulness depend heavily on understanding the intent of the audience.

To capitalize on relevancy and intent as a marketer, remember these four query types:

- Informational
- Investigative
- Navigational
- Transactional

Each of these query types can be associated with certain phases of the consumer purchase journey:

Informational Queries – Researching non-transactional information

Informational queries are at the very top of the funnel – the awareness phase. Results are usually broad and informative, with no intent to sell. The main intent behind informational queries is, well, to get information. Most search results associated with informational queries tend to be direct answers.

Investigative Queries – Researching options

Investigative queries come from consumers with the intention to discover options in the market or do additional research. In terms of the consumer purchase process, these searchers can be in either the awareness or consideration phases of the funnel. These queries may not necessarily lead to conversions. Indeed, they may not even be driven by any intent to purchase.

These are queries that involve researching specific details. Searchers may be looking for talent, competition or options available in the market.

The intention behind these queries may or may not be to eventually purchase, but what Google does know (or assumes) is that the searcher is exploring options. Search results are, therefore, tailored to provide those options for investigation.

- -

Navigational Queries – Looking for something you already know you want

By this phase, the consumer already knows what they want. Perhaps it is healthy fruits (from informational queries) and the consumer now knows the best places to buy them (investigative queries).

In navigational queries, when the searcher knows the brand, product or service name, but does not know the URL, they will just type the name into their search or address bar.

For example, when you want to access Gmail, you usually just type "Gmail" into the address bar rather than a full URL. Google does the rest because it assumes (from what you're currently typing and from your past behaviour) that your intent is to navigate to your Gmail account.

As generations are getting lazier by the second, navigational queries are becoming more and more popular.

Transactional Queries are queries that involve an intent towards an action

The action doesn't have to be money related. It could be a signup, newsletter, phone details, address discovery, getting directions... in search queries, these are all considered "transactions".

For example, if you search "Buy healthy food", that is considered a transactional query. Likewise, if you search "Gmail registration", that is also considered transactional.

So, what can we do as marketers, entrepreneurs, and startups?

We have to capitalize on the searcher's intent instead of simply keywords, and strive to capitalize on each query type.

I would recommend using this approach in your future content as well as to modify and optimize past content. Go to your current blogs, pages, and product pages. Analyze the actual intent and value of the content (meaning what someone is likely to do with, or get from, the content) and update accordingly.

The best way to test search intent is Google Search itself. Search the term you have in mind and, based on the search results you get, you will be able to categorize it accordingly. Let's say you're running an organic produce market in Montreal. Search the term "organic vegetables Montreal". Where does your site come up (if at all)? What are the top results? What are they doing that you might be missing? How can you optimize your site to build up your ranking for that term?

Remember that there are no right or wrong search intent queries. The right approach is to match the right queries with your brand and business goals. If you are an e-commerce site, it is ideal to concentrate on transactional queries and investigation queries, while not fully ignoring the informational and navigational queries.

Intentions can no longer be ignored; they need to be a critical part of your marketing moving forward.

Sources:

https://moz.com/blog/segmenting-search-intent

http://searchengineland.com/search-intent-signals-aligning-organic-paid-search-strategy-249601

Takeaway

SEO and digital marketing provide the unique opportunity of being able to market to user intent. To capitalize on this, pay attention to the four types of queries: informational, investigative, navigational and transactional. Work these into your SEO and digital marketing strategies.

Chapter 8

SEO & Content

The Ultimate SEO Content Checklist

SEO has changed a lot in recent years and will continue to change in the years ahead.

Search engines are getting smarter, users are changing how they search, and search engine specialists are pushed to stay on top of their game. But one thing remains of huge importance to SEO: content. Content will always be king. It's just how we approach that content that must continually evolve as the people and search engines accessing it evolve.

With that in mind, here is your ultimate SEO content checklist for killer content:

1. Addressing Searcher Intent vs. Just the Keywords

This cannot be stressed enough: INTENT over keywords. Whatever words or phrases someone types into a search bar, there is always an intent behind it. There is a goal; a type of content they hope to find.

Keywords do matter, so include them, but do it organically, address intent first, and remember the four types of search intent: informative, investigative, navigational and transactional.

2. Answer Questions

More and more, people are searching as if they're speaking. For example, if someone wants to know how to create a mobile app, they're far more likely to search "how to create a mobile app" than "mobile app creation." This is partly due to the growth in voice search, but also happening in typed searches.

In fact, we're moving more and more towards question-style searches as the years progress.

As you build your content strategy, ensure you are directly answering questions and optimize your content for question-style searches.

---

3. Create Original Content

When I ask other experts in the field about the best backlinking strategies ("backlinking" meaning getting other sites to link to you), **the most common answer is to be original and create unique content.**

Original content is important for both search engines and humans. Regardless of any positive impact on backlinking, it is your safest bet to not get penalized for duplicate content.

---

4. Create Content with Google's Mission in Mind

You need to think about searchers' intent, but also Google's intent. Their mission is to organize the world's information and make it universally accessible and useful.

Google will always evolve towards their mission. So, make your content accessible, useful and linkable, and Google will reward you.

---

5. Create Engaging Content

Google knows how engaging your content is, and rewards it.

As of this book's writing, the main ranking factors for search engines are all user related: time spent on site, bounce rate, pages per visit, etc. All these metrics relate to users and how engaged they are on your site.
Make content people want to spend time with.

---

6. Diversify!

Video, images, text, gifs... product descriptions, reviews, helpful tips, useful articles, fun facts, media coverage, quizzes, your grandmother's famous sugar cookie recipe... Is it relevant? Is it fun? Accessible? Linkable? Useful? Engaging? **Get it up there! Diversify your content and your content type. Users like it, Google likes it.**

---

7. Create for Humans

Never create just for search engines. Never feel like you owe your SEO expert a list of keywords in your content or title tag or anything.

Yes, search engines will see it first. But it's the human interaction that matters most. Create for humans because no matter how optimized your content is for the engines, if people don't spend time with it, the engines will stop noticing.

---

8. Be Legit and Make Sense

Search engines are getting smart. Really smart. Like, robot-overlords-are-not-that-far-off smart.

Let's say I'm writing about "the best neighbourhoods in Montreal". Google will actually grade my authority and article integrity based on if I reference actual neighbourhoods, such as NDG, St-Henri, Jean Talon, etc...

Google knows that these are legit neighbourhoods and will look for them. If it doesn't find any, the article is not deemed worthy.

---

9. Check Your Grammar

Despite the valiant efforts of far too many people, "your" and "you're" still are not interchangeable.

As part of evolving search engine intelligence, they are also getting sensitive to our (perceived) intelligence. There is a level of credibility associated with proper grammar and search engines know that. Check your grammar. Twice.

---

10. Ensure Structural Integrity

Structured sites lead to structured content. Working on your site with structure in mind pays off by keeping you safe from cannibalization.

Categorize and tag your site so that you address all topics in a niche and granulated manner.

Takeaway

Search is all about finding good, relevant, accessible content. What you put out there and how you put it out there matters. A lot.

Are SEO and Content Marketing Supposed to be Separate?

>>>

Should we be treating our Search Engine Marketing and content marketing projects with different strategies?

I get a lot of client calls asking the same question, which is normal. But, a more specific question is, where do we draw the line between content and SEO?

The problem is this:

Most of these clients, currently and historically, seem to hire two different agencies: one for SEO, and one for content marketing. In a situation like this, the creative agency will be the one with less technical skills, and with a lot of content writing experience, while the SEO agency will be more technically oriented.

Solution:

Clients and agencies should work together to integrate SEO and content marketing efforts. Content truly is king as it has huge influence over the success of your SEO efforts. Trying to keep content and SEO separate will put you at a disadvantage. The benefits of marrying search engine tags with content will yield a bigger reward and a higher ROI. If you have no choice but to use separate agencies, try to get them working together and aligning your strategies.

―――――――――――――――――――――――――――――

3 important points on this matter:

Successful SEO is done with both the content and the client in mind.

Successful SEO is created with real human readers as the audience, not bots.

Successful content marketing embraces SEO, completely.

―――――――――――――――――――――――――――――

What should you know as a marketer or business owner?

Content marketing is a great way to establish trust, authority and build strong relationships with clients and partners. It will help position you as an expert in your field.

Most people will come across your brand with a question they want answered. Make sure you are there for them with the right information, listed and categorized.

How will they find you?
    1. Through search engines
    2. Social searches/social timelines

How will you rank?
    1. By using good content
    2. Using the right content in the right spots
    3. Tagging the right content with the right tags
    4. Getting the right (adequate search volume) keywords to best describe your content

How to stay ranking?
    1. Use engaging content; content that will keep people on your pages for more than just 10 seconds
    2. Use visuals, infographics, graphs, pics, etc.
    3. Use videos
    4. Use strong references

What can content and SEO build together?

Remember one of the most important ranking factors in SEO: time spent on site. When people spend time with your content, search engines reward you. When people arrive on your site and leave within seconds, search engines take note of that as well. And not favourably.

Lean on your SEO resources to identify the best keywords to target, then create useful, engaging, valuable content from them, then go back to your SEO resources to ensure everything is tagged and structured appropriately. This is how you transform your marketing strategy into a more successful mix.

Takeaway:

It is important for all of us to start looking at SEO and content as allies and not rivals.

These two should work together as there is unlikely to be any point in the future when one will replace the other.

What is likely is that content will continue to drift towards the technical, while SEO continues to drift towards the resourceful and creative. Focus on both as a combined strategy and you'll be well prepared for the present and the future.

Resources/Sources:
https://blog.kissmetrics.com/seo-is-content-marketing/
http://www.searchenginejournal.com/combine-seo-content-marketing-explosive-results/97157/
http://searchengineland.com/content-marketing-seo-bigger-picture-219796
http://www.searchenginejournal.com/combine-seo-content-marketing-explosive-results/97157/

Chapter 9

Local SEO

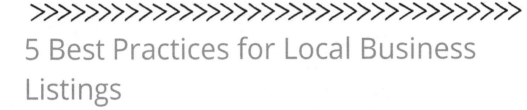

5 Best Practices for Local Business Listings

Eight years into my journey as a digital marketer, I have developed a habit of assessing the local listings of any place I show up to.

Every time I go to a restaurant, coffee shop or retail store in a rural area, I do an assessment of the business's local listings. I make it my mission to help out, as my drive to be a supportive digital marketer kicks in.

What has become apparent in recent years is that, no matter how small the community, online local listings and local business strength are increasingly important. Even your neighbour is pulling up listings on their smartphone and that is impacting their purchasing decisions. Yes, even if your business is right next door.

In going from place to place, assessing listings as I go, I have noticed several trends in how businesses handle (or don't handle) their local listings.

Here are 5 of my top observations, and what you can do about them:

1. Google is not everything

As important as your Google listing is, you will still have considerable traffic coming from other listings and search engines.

Here are the top traffic drivers that you should be aware of:
- Google My Business – https://www.google.com/business/
- Bing Places – https://www.bingplaces.com
- Yelp – https://biz.yelp.com

- Yellow Pages – http://m1.adsolutions.yp.com/free-listing-basic-benefits
- FourSquare – http://business.foursquare.com
- Whitepages – https://www.whitepages.com

These services are all free and can potentially drive significant traffic. If you have not properly set up your listings on these services, it would be in your best interests to do so or find someone (like a digital marketer) who can do it for you.

---

2. Make sure your listings are complete

What constitutes a complete listing is different from one platform to another. Yet, there are some basic elements that should be included in each and every listing, across all platforms:

- Name
- Tagline
- Description
- Address
- Phone
- Site URL
- Hours of operation
- Categories
- Photos and videos

Then there are a few "nice to have" elements:

- Alternate phone numbers
- Social channels
- Payment methods accepted

Make sure all your listings are as complete as possible.

3. Make sure your listings are consistent (down to the letter!)

The key to successful local SEO is consistency. Accurate and consistent information across all your listings will improve your SEO reputation, which is an important factor in how well you rank in search results.

For example, Google has a measurement index called "listing accuracy". This index relies on the consistency of your information across these listings.

Do an audit of your online listings, including everywhere in your own website and/or blog that lists such information. Ensure all information is consistent, down to the letter, with your current business status.

4. Avoid duplicate listings

Having more than one listing with different information is a red flag to Google and other search engines that your data is not accurate.

Also, since search engines pull information from many different sources, duplicate listings will dilute your ranking position (i.e. you may rank lower in search results pages).

Did you or someone in your business accidentally submit two listings to Yellow Pages, for example? Make sure there is only one and that it has accurate and consistent information.

5. Get REAL reviews

There is nothing more discrediting than seeing a local listing with 10 reviews, all of them 5/5 and all of them left by people with the same family name. It's nice to have a supportive family, but it's important to get impartial, authentic reviews as well.

When in the pursuit of reviews, make sure that you are inviting your actual clients to leave reviews and not just family members. This authenticity really does matter to potential clients or customers.

Also, make sure that you are up to date! If you change your business hours, your location, storefront, phone number or any other essential details, make sure to update your listings as well.

Takeaway

Local listings are used to ensure that your visitors find your business. View this as a positive thing and use it to your advantage.

Drive value in the best possible ways by providing relevant, up to date and consistent information about your business.

For local businesses to thrive, online marketing is a must. Searching online is now the number one-way people find the products, services and businesses they're looking for. You need to make sure they're finding you and getting the most relevant information when they do.

Chapter 10

SEO & Keyword Research

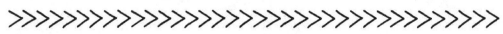

Use Trend Measurement Tools
3 Trend Measurement Tools Your Business Needs

Wouldn't it be great to have the inside track on the next big thing? Or insight into what's going to grab your market's attention? Once you knew that, the question would be how to capitalize on that insight.

Trend management tools can be a bit like crystal balls, but based on data, not fantasy. Beyond insight into the future, they also help you plan for the future. As entrepreneurs, we all want to predict the future. In the past, we used historical data and, essentially, educated guessing to determine future trends. That left a large margin for error and, with today's faster pace of change, historical data isn't always a reliable predictor of the future.

Trend measurement tools are making future predictions much more accurate, because they use real-time data input, and can aggregate data from multiple sources, across multiple platforms and enable you to quickly analyze, compare and understand the data in many different ways. These tools really do give you an edge in the market.

There are four key factors that make trend measurement tools vital to success:

1. Understanding trends empowers you to leverage every growth opportunity and each moment your competition might be missing.

2. Trends help you prepare for downturns. Knowing about a market slump in advance lets you better prepare for it, which can be just as valuable as being able to capitalize on upturns.

3. Trends give you insight into how often people search for your brand vs competitors, so you can understand the lows and highs of the

competition and plan accordingly.

4. Trends provide insight into your industry overall. If you're just starting a business, this helps you enter the market strategically. If you're up and running, it enables you to tailor content to your market and adjust that content as the market changes.

So, what trend management tools will give you what you need? Our good friend Google actually provides three powerful (and free, at least as of this writing) tools that can be used for trend management.

The Best (Free) Tools

Tool #1 - Google Trends

Let's imagine you are a headphones company and want to capitalize on peak interest throughout the year.

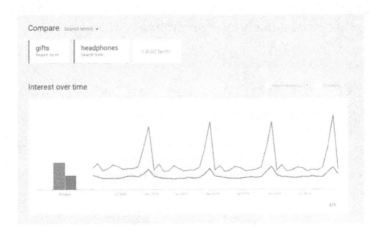

Google Trends can show you a year over year trend for the term "gifts" and a similar trend for "headphones", co-occurring during the December/January holiday period.

However, as you can see in the chart above, there are also three additional opportunities around Valentine's Day, Father's Day and Mother's Day. Once we have that insight, we can act accordingly to capitalize on these untapped market trends. An example could be, "An Unconventional Gift for an Unconventional Dad". Create content targeted to these untapped trends and you are uniquely placed to capitalize on them.

Start typing in Google. What do you see? A bunch of autocomplete suggestions and related topics. Helpful when you're looking for something.... SUPER helpful to know what others are looking for! Although this is more of a feature than a standalone tool, there is a wealth of insight to be gleaned from the results.

Here's an example:

Imagine you are a real estate start-up running out of blog ideas. You need to fill up your editorial calendar.

Type "5 things to consider before moving out" into Google. It's a broad topic and hard to rank on for SEO, but related topics have more potential. Take a look at the autocomplete suggestions:

It's not only a ready-made list of related topics to write about, but you now know that these are things people are actively searching for.

Next, look at the related searches at the bottom of the page:

Searches related to 5 things to consider before moving out

things to consider before moving in with someone

things to consider before moving in together

things to consider before moving in with boyfriend

things to consider before moving in with your boyfriend

things to consider before moving to a new city

things to consider when moving out on your own

things to consider when moving out for the first time

things to consider when moving out of state

Yet another ready-made list to inspire blog posts, articles, newsletters and much more. And again, since these results are driven by what other people are searching for, if you build content around them, you know you're creating something that provides real value. This is far more than guessing or taking a shot in the dark. This is data-driven strategy.

The fact that this data is coming directly from Google AND that it provides insight into what users want is hugely advantageous from an SEO perspective. Remember, Google's mission is usefulness and accessibility for the user. Our mission as SEO experts is to create for the user, not the search engines... so that search engines take note of how useful and accessible we are. This insight into what people are actually searching for allows us to hit that nail square on the head.

Tool #3 - Google AdWords/Google Ads

What? AdWords isn't free! Well, you do have to pay for ads, but an AdWords account is free and comes with the handy (and free) Keyword Tool, which finds related trends and measures their search volume. With a free AdWords account, you get full access to this tool and its powerful features.

Keyword	Avg. Monthly Se	Competition
things to consider when moving out of state	110	0.22
things to consider before moving in together	**90**	**0.01**
things to consider before moving in with your boyfriend	40	0
things to consider when moving out for the first time	**30**	**0.02**
things to consider before moving in with someone		
things to consider before moving in with boyfriend		
things to consider before moving to a new city		
things to consider when moving out on your own		

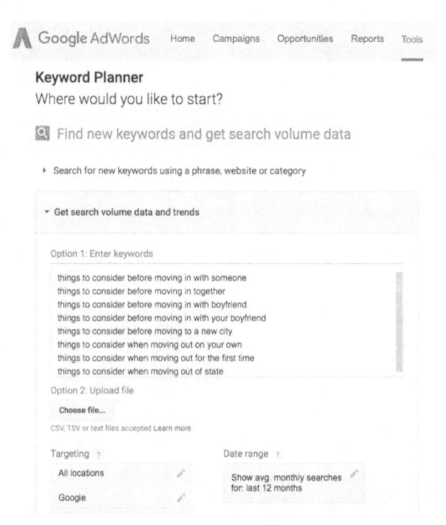

Using terms from our real estate example, you can see that the first 4 topics are most worth writing about, based on average monthly searches.

But take a look at the second column - Competition. AdWords operates on a bidding model, with advertisers bidding on different keywords and phrases to get their ads displayed. The Competition column you see above indicates the level of competitiveness for each phrase, giving you an idea of what competing businesses are focusing their efforts on. So, what you're really seeing is opportunities to get a leg up on the competition. As you can see above, rows 2 and 4 are extremely relevant to our real estate business and have low competition. These are two great trends to write about!

Two topics are great, more is better. So now you want to find more related topics. Still using Keyword Tool, use the option to search for new keywords using phrase, website or category.

B	C	D	E
Keyword	Currency	Avg. Monthly Se	Competition
things to consider before moving in together	CAD	90	0.01
things to consider when moving out for the first tim	CAD	30	0.02
moving in together	CAD	5400	0.02
moving out	CAD	9900	0.06
moving out of home	CAD	1000	0.18
moving out for the first time	CAD	1600	0.03
first apartment	CAD	2900	0.08
first time renter	CAD	720	0.33
move in	CAD	9900	0.06
moving out of home for the first time	CAD	170	0.13
checklist for moving out	CAD	260	0.25
moving out list	CAD	320	0.14
moving in together checklist	CAD	320	0.13
things to do when moving	CAD	590	0.22
cost of moving out	CAD	210	0.16
moving out checklist	CAD	2900	0.22
moving out expenses	CAD	90	0.32
first time moving out	CAD	260	0.04
my first apartment	CAD	1300	0.16
first time apartment renter	CAD	260	0.41
list for moving out	CAD	90	0.24
first time apartment	CAD	210	0.21

You now have 380 keywords, for which you know the volume and competition.

As you build or grow your business, keep these tools handy. Use them when planning promotions, email campaigns, blog posts or any marketing content. They will give your business a serious edge.

The best way to explain how these tools work is through the below example of capitalizing on your off-season.

Example

>>>

Learning Through Example

How to Capitalize on Your Company's Off-Season

Most companies and startups tend to give less attention to the low season compared to the high season. Yet, in this day and age, if you are not present and active at all times, you are dead in the water.

Recognizing Your Off-Season

You probably have a good idea of your off-season, but there's a saying in data analytics (and life) - numbers don't lie. I would add to that, the more numbers you have, the clearer a picture of the truth you have. You may be basing your understanding of off-season on sales or traffic, for example, but what about search?

One of the best ways to predict when your off-season is, is to research search trends surrounding your product. To do so, look at both general industry trends and your own unique search trends through Google Analytics. Google Analytics is a free data analytics tool that provides valuable insight into the performance of web properties. It is a must-have tool for any business with a website, and hugely beneficial in planning, running, tracking and optimizing a successful SEO strategy.

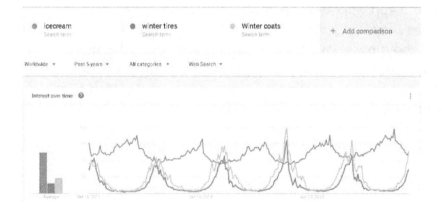

In the graph above, I selected three products (ice cream, winter tires, winter coats) that are all highly seasonal, and entered them as potential search terms. By simply comparing the three charted lines you can begin to see how seasonal changes can dramatically influence the demand for a product from one month to another.

These graphs, provided by Google Trends, will also allow you to understand user search behaviour from before, during, and after your high season. Equipped with this information, you can understand user-demand from an annual perspective and plan accordingly.

- -

Now That You Know Your Off-Season, How Can You Handle It?

Use the time for buildup, preparation and collecting leads for your high season.

If there's one important thing that I've learned with seasonal products and services, it's that you have to prepare for your off-season during your high season and prepare for your high season during your off-season.

During your high season, try to remember that, just as it is in the movie industry, the buildup is everything. So, as you are marketing for the high season, remember to collect as many leads, emails and followers as possible to cover your entire year.

Make sure that you appropriately market to these leads throughout the off-season in order to keep you and your product at the top of their minds. You don't want to be scrambling with branding and awareness campaigns, or struggling with low search rankings right before a peak. Instead, you want to have laid the groundwork for strong brand recognition and search rankings, so that you can take full advantage of the high season.

Never Underestimate the Off-Season Market. Don't Stop Your Marketing in the Downtime.

Never assume the off-season is a time to relax. During off-season, the market is usually much less saturated and the competition is less active. Use this to your advantage and push all forms of advertising throughout the off-season.

There is always a market that is not tapped into or is under-utilized. If you understand trends and consumer behaviour, you will be able to associate occasions (a specific time of year for your product) no matter how "off season" they may be.

I recommend creating a marketing calendar up to a year ahead of time. Come up with new content every week (either a blog, video, podcast, etc.) and, on a larger scale, create a new campaign or event to invite people to every 45 days or so. Keeping your content fresh, even during your off season, will help build and preserve strong search rankings over time.

Remember, SEO isn't a standalone tactic and it isn't a one-and-done tactic either. It's a consistent strategy combining multiple channels with the aim of keeping users engaged, in order to strengthen SEO success.

Now, you may be thinking, "How on earth would you market winter coats during the off-season?" You could create content around proper cleaning and storage of winter garments (great for capitalizing on all those "spring cleaning" search terms), create funny videos of staff trying to "test" coats in the summer (maybe holding a staff meeting inside a walk-in freezer), you could sponsor a charity event, or even partner with a business whose high season is summer in some unique way. Get creative and keep value and authenticity top of mind. Just remember that there can be value in humour, and a lot of humour to be found in juxtaposition.

Whether it be with an eBook, webinar, public speaking event, or anything else, the fact is, when you plan your calendar year accordingly, you are continuously coming up with new content and events to grow your network. And a larger network will help minimize your off-time purely by volume of users, and keep your search rankings healthy by providing those key metrics search engines are looking for - time spent on site, page views per visit, etc.

Trying, Measuring, Analyzing, and Updating

Never forget TMAU! Try, measure, analyze and update. All aspects of marketing, including SEO, have always been about trying, not about being perfect. It is always about testing out new approaches, new tricks, new creatives, new algorithms, etc. It's a constantly changing balancing act of try, measure, analyze and update.

What works now may not work in the next few weeks, months, or years. The only way to stay ahead of the game is by continuously trying new things. Your off-season is the perfect opportunity to test. Test website elements, landing pages, newsletter components... test everything, measure, analyze, update, then test again. Get all aspects of your business and marketing optimized and ready to take your next high season even higher.

Stay Active, Be Present, Be Helpful and Be Supportive.

Above all, don't disappear. Your off-season is a good time to do behind the scenes TMAU work, but don't ignore your audience in the process. Keep your social media active. Keep your newsletter going. Keep adding new content, hosting events, giving promotions. Get creative, use the trend management tools, and find ways to be relevant, supportive, helpful, present and active. Your target audience will notice, which means search engines will notice as well.

Takeaway

Staying active, resourceful and present at all times, even during your off season, whether it be on social media, blogs, forums, etc. is key to a successful SEO strategy. Not only will regularly engaging with your user-base help build a great reputation, create loyalty and strengthen search rankings, it will also differentiate you from your competition. No matter the time of year, always make time for your users, and the effort will pay off.

And remember, use more than one tool to get your data. Don't rely on only one source.

Chapter 11

Keyword Mapping

>>>

Try, Measure, Analyze and Update

When it comes to SEO, most people know that keywords are an important element. And they are. But they're only one part of an overall strategy, and they need to be used carefully and with user intent in mind.

The first step is to conduct your keyword research. This is where you identify the words and terms (most "keywords" are actually terms consisting of 2, 3 or even more words) related to your business, product or service that people are actually using to conduct searches online.

In the previous chapter, we looked at a few methods of conducting keyword research using trend management tools to identify terms that people are actually searching for. For keyword research, you want to start off with several broad terms related to your business, then use the tools to identify the more targeted keywords worth working to rank for. Using the tools is important. You may have an idea of keywords that seem obvious to you, but... are actual humans using those exact words and terms? The tools will tell you. They will also tell you if a keyword is too competitive to aim for right out of the gate. Start by aiming for less competitive keywords to build a strong reputation with search engines, and with your audience.

After you have done your keyword research, you ideally want to choose two keywords for each page of your website. These keywords will be known as your primary and secondary KWs (KW = keyword).

It is important that you choose specific keywords for each page on the site. If pages are using very similar terms or if the same terms are being used across the site, it will cause the site to cannibalize itself. This is also known as 'keyword cannibalization'.

Choosing these specific keywords for each page is what's known as keyword mapping - mapping out your researched keywords to their respective pages based on what is most relevant.

Let's look at an example:

I run a blog called Montreal Tips where I put together articles about Montreal - businesses, restaurants, activities, festivals, neighborhoods, etc.

The mission and purpose of Montreal Tips is to support ideas, entrepreneurs, start-ups, businesses, causes and local talent, helping them succeed while helping Montrealer's and tourists discover new businesses, activities and experiences.

Let's say we are writing an article on "The Best Lebanese Restaurants in Montreal."

After doing some keyword research, as was done in the previous chapter, we discover the ideal terms to go with:

-   Top Lebanese food Restos
-   Lebanese food in Montreal

We choose these because a decent number of people search these terms regularly, the competition is fairly low, we don't have any other pages/articles targeting these terms (avoiding cannibalization), and content around these terms will provide value to our readers (remember: create with the user in mind first!).

To put this article in a keyword map, here is what it would look like:

Page/Topic	KW 1	KW 2
"The Best Lebanese Restaurants in Montreal."	Top Lebanese food Restos	Lebanese food in Montreal

This would be part of a larger document mapping all of our keywords across all of our pages. Why do we record it? Again, it's to avoid keyword cannibalization. In practice, we can't be expected to remember the keywords targeted on every single page. Also, if you have multiple people working on content, or if you bring in someone new mid-project, you need to be able to share this information with everyone involved.

Now... is this enough? No.

Related Terms

Once again, we have evolving search engine intelligence to contend with. It is no longer enough to rely only on keywords. Our content has to make sense to both the user and the search engines. Search engines are armed with almost all the knowledge on the internet, which means they have the information needed to determine if our content is credible or not. This is where related terms come in.

Let's imagine we are writing an article about five neighborhoods to visit in Montreal.

Google takes note of the word "neighborhoods". Google also knows the names of all the neighborhoods in Montreal and will expect actual neighborhoods to be mentioned. If they aren't, Google will deem the article as not credible.

To make sure we include terms Google can use to determine our credibility, I strongly recommend including related terms in the keyword map. So, if we are talking about neighborhoods in Montreal, Google is expecting to see terms like:

- Montreal Downtown
- NDG - Notre-Dame-de-Grâce
- Mile End
- Le Plateau-Mont-Royal
- Gay Village
- Mont-Royal
- Westmount
- Etc...

Page/Topic	KW 1	KW 2	Related Terms
"5 Neighborhoods to visit in Montreal"	Montreal famous neighborhoods	Places to walk in Montreal	- Montreal Downtown -NDG - Notre-Dame-de-Grâce -Mile End -Mile X -Little Italy -Le Plateau-Mont-Royal -Gay Village -Griffintown -Mont-Royal -Westmount -Old Montreal

Questions to be Answered

On the note of search engines getting better and better, smarter and smarter, it's important to recognize and keep in mind that they are doing so in their mission to drive value to users.

Meaning, if we are not bringing value to our users, we are not valuable to search engines.

To be valuable to users, we have to provide answers to their questions.

Although not all search terms are framed as questions, that's essentially what they all are. That said, our search behaviour has changed a lot in that we are more often searching the way we speak or think, and search terms are becoming more question-like.

For example, if we are looking for a restaurant near us, we will type in the query, "Restaurants near me". If we are looking for a fast way to transfer money, we will type, "What is the fastest way to transfer money?".

This is true now more than ever as voice search is becoming more and more popular.

Because of this, it's becoming necessary for us to include questions in our keyword mapping approach.

To do this, I have been using an amazing tool called Answer the Public. Although I've nicknamed it 'the grumpy old man tool'.

This tool gives you all the possible variations of all the questions being asked by the general public. All you have to do is input the topic that you have in mind.

Answer the public tool: https://answerthepublic.com/
Snapshot: Front page of https://answerthepublic.com/

After you input your term, Answer the Public will provide you will the list of questions associated with it. Add this tool to the trend management tools discussed earlier, and you'll be all set for top notch keyword research.

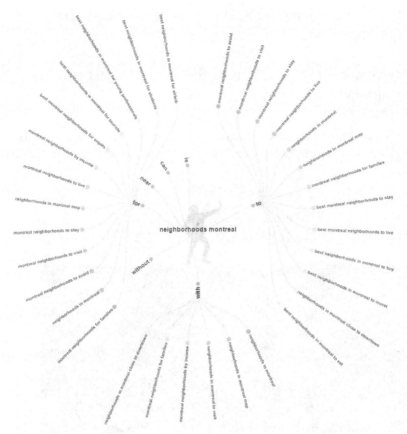

Figure 12.1 - Source: answerthepublic.com

Takeaway

As search engine algorithms get more sophisticated, our SEO strategies must follow suit. Stuffing keywords throughout your pages just won't cut it. Put the work in. Do the research. Put real strategy into your keyword approach. That work will pay off.

Chapter 12

On Page Tags

On page optimization" is exactly what it sounds like - the optimizations that you do directly on (or within) the pages of your site. These optimizations include creating content, how you structure the site, your keyword mapping, etc. They also include most of the on-page tags of the website.

What are the on-page tags that we can optimize?

- Meta title tags
- Meta descriptions
- Page URLs
- Content on page
- Alt text for images

A tag is essentially a descriptor within your page. It's data about your data. So, where an image on your page would be part of the page data or content, the alt image text is the data about that content, and is considered a tag. It is important that the work we do on these tags is aligned with the keyword map that we put together in the previous chapter.

Meta Title Tags

HTML: <title>Page title goes here</title>

A meta title tag is the first thing that you see in search results.
In the example below, the meta title tag is "5 Best National Parks Near Montreal | Top 5 National Parks in Quebec"

5 Best National Parks Near Montreal | Top 5 National Parks in Quebec
https://montrealtips.com/2018/02/06/5-best-national-parks-near-montreal/   ▾
Feb 6, 2018 - First, a little note on "**national**" **parks**. Across Canada, there are many parks protected, preserved and maintained by Parks Canada. These are ...

Going by the Moz recommendations - https://moz.com/learn/seo/title-tag - we should ideally use both our primary keyword and secondary keyword, alongside our brand name in the title:

Primary Keyword - Secondary Keyword | Brand Name

If we go back to the keyword map that we put together in the previous chapter, here is how the title would look:

Page/Topic	KW 1	KW 2	Related Terms
"5 Neighborhoods to visit in Montreal"	Montreal Famous Neighborhoods	Places to walk in Montreal	-Montreal Downtown -NDG - Notre-Dame-de-Grâce -Mile End -Le Plateau-Mont-Royal -Gay Village -Mont-Royal -Westmount
Title	Montreal Famous Neighborhoods	Places to walk in Montreal		

It is important to note that the title should be under 65 characters. More than that and the full title won't show in search results. Instead, it would be cut off with three dots at the end.

Montreal Famous Neighborhoods | Places to walk in Montreal | ...

Figure 21.1 - Three dots at the end of the title

Meta Descriptions

The meta description is often shown under the meta title in Google search results. Google will show up to 160 characters for this part. When no meta description is available, search engines will often take the first 160 characters of text on that page.

Meta description actually no longer has a direct impact on a page's SEO. Yet, it does have an indirect impact.

What does that mean?

For search engines right now, the most important ranking factors are user behaviour related. Meaning CTR (click through rate) and number of visits, for example.

So, while the meta description won't directly impact SEO, it can have a direct impact on user behaviour, which will have a direct impact on SEO. If people are drawn in by the description and click on your search result, that tells Google that your search result is valuable to users. Kudos to you!

What does that tell us as marketers?

When we are creating a description for our site, it is more important that we create the descriptions with user engagement, than with search engines, in mind.

It is definitely important to include consistent keywords, as consistency is important to user experience, but it is also important to have a call to action and content that pique's the searcher's interest.

Page URLs

Earlier in the book, we mentioned the importance of site structure. Good site structure means having a clean and well-organized site, which leads to a good URL structure.

What I tell my students at Concordia University is the following: "I should be able to understand what the site is about, what the page is about, and where it fits by just looking at your URL."

When creating URLs, always bear that in mind. Also bear in mind what you should NOT use:

- o **Capital Letters**: having different letter cases in a URL makes a URL inconsistent. It will also dilute your page strength as this will create a different version of it. Always keep your URLs in lower case.

- o **Underscores**: The reason is that search engines and browsers view underscores as nothing, but hyphens as spaces. So, if a search engine sees this in the URL - "best_montreal_restos_for_date" - it will read it as "bestmontrealrestosfordate". Instead, use hyphens: "best-montreal-restos-for-date". Google will read the hyphens as spaces and identify each word separately.

- o **NON-ASCII characters**: ASCII stands for American Standard Code for Information Interchange. Since URLs can only communicate using ASCII characters, when they see a non-ASCII character, they replace it with a "%" sign, which causes URL issues and broken pages in the long run. You can Google a table of ASCII characters to check that your URLs are compliant.

- o **Spaces**: Avoid spaces at all costs, if you leave a space when you are creating a URL, it will convert that space into a "%20" when the site is live. That also causes the URL to have issues and might negatively affect your SEO. It's also a terrible user experience.

On Page Content

It just can't be said enough. Content is king.

SEO and on page content go hand in hand. Based on research by SEMrush, sites that rank number one for their targeted keywords have, on average, 45% more content than sites ranking 20th.

Using the right content - impactful, useful, engaging - on your site will help a lot.

Put it this way: if Google doesn't know enough about you, they will be looking to see if you are an expert on your subject. The more content you give, the better, and the more you can prove you are knowledgeable on the subject, the better.

When it comes to content, the quantity of content is as important as the quality of content. As you fill up your site with content, make sure it is as meaningful and valuable as possible, and tap every resource you can for new ideas for fresh, useful and unique content.

Alt Text for Images

Alt image tags are made first and foremost for the visually impaired.

When someone with visual impairment is checking out your site, they will be able to know what the image is about by moving their mouse over it, and having their screen-reader software read out the alt text.

As this is the main purpose, we shouldn't look at this tag primarily from an SEO perspective, but from an ethical and purposeful perspective. Creating these tags to be meaningful and useful is not only a best practice, but our duty and responsibility. See example:

ALT tag: A large scale mural of Leonard Cohen on the side of a building in downtown Montreal, Quebec, Canada.

The alt text for this image is useful, relevant and fulfils its purpose of making content more accessible. Remember the two most important words of Google's mission? Useful and accessible! Be useful and be accessible. It's what Google wants, it's what users want and it's what will bolster the credibility of your site for both.

Takeaway

In terms of SEO, on page tags no longer have the direct impact they once did. However, they can have a strong indirect impact. Since search engines prioritize user metrics, indirect impacts are incredibly important for the digital marketer. Don't neglect these elements simply because their value has evolved. Always, always, always optimize with the user in mind.

Chapter 13

SEO and Site Migrations

SEO Friendly Site Migration

Tips on Conducting a Site Migration Without Losing Rankings, Traffic and SEO Strength

- -

Site migration is the process where you move a site to a new domain or directory. It can happen for a number of reasons, such as a change in company name requiring a new URL.

Migrating happens to almost every company out there, and more often than we tend to realize.

All marketers and digital specialists aspire and aim for a site migration that does not create any loss in traffic, revenue, SERP rank, or SEO strength. What I hear most often is that it is as simple as redirecting the old domain to the new domain using a 301 redirect – this is an SEO friendly type of redirect. A 301 redirect tells search engines that the content has simply moved and where to find the new location. This is a good start and better than nothing. But it is important to follow a more detailed procedure that will allow you to make this transition without losing value, while getting rid of any mistakes on the current site.

So, how do you accomplish this? There is a three-phase process and three steps to prepare for that process.

Step 1 is understanding the objective behind an SEO friendly migration.

The main goals to keep in mind are:
1. Maintain traffic
2. Maintain rankings
3. Seamless user experience and transition

Step 2 is to know what to pay attention to.

Understand that there is no magic bullet. we need to do the best we can to ensure that we maintain the highest ranking possible.

Here are the main factors to pay extra attention to:
1. URL structure
2. Duplicate content
3. Canonicalization
4. Indexed pages

Step 3 is to fully understand the process.

Here are the 3 phases of an SEO friendly site migration:
1. Premigration
2. Migration
3. Post-migration

Phase 1: Pre-Migration

Here is what to account for and work on:

Know what you have on your current site/platform

For an ideal SEO friendly site migration, the best place to start is with an SEO audit of the current site, as it is important not to bring the current site's mistakes with you to the new one.

Understand and map current site architecture

Download your current sitemaps and export the list of indexed pages from the Google Search Console. This will give you a full list of all pages to be redirected to the new site, and prevent any oversights. Remember that SEO is holistic - it's about the full picture. All of your pages work together to build overall site strength. If one gets overlooked in a migration, any value that page was providing gets lost.

Understand and map new site architecture

Create a full map of what your new site will look like - all the pages and their new URLs. This will come in handy when creating your URL redirect map.

Create a URL redirect map

Map out all the old URLs to the new URLs on the new site. If you have pages on the old site that you don't want to carry over, you still need to redirect those URLs somewhere. Otherwise, you risk ending up with broken links (on your own site, or on external sites linking to you) and losing all the great SEO strength built up by those links. A best practice is to identify a page on the new site that best compl*ements the content on the old site and redirect the old URL to that one.*

Account for technical limitations

In some situations of moving domains, directories, or hosting, it is important to understand if the new site can support all the changes being made. Look into this beforehand so you can plan (or alter plans) accordingly.

Additional Factors to Account For:

URL structure

Ensure the new site is well structured and categorized, so that there is consistency across all the pages, posts and properties.

Content – avoid duplication

Ensure you are using the right tags on the new site to avoid any duplicate content.

Messaging/New design/Site

With migrations, we often work for a long time on the new design and URL before the migration ever takes place. As such, we tend to forget that our users don't share our familiarity. The change will be totally new to them. It is important to have a notification mentioning the changes and if it will affect your visitors/users in any way.

Smart marketers see the opportunity in this and turn new designs and domains into marketing advantages. They create buildup, set a release date, request feedback, and plan for an exciting launch.

Phase 2: Migration Process

Keep the old site (in parallel while using the right redirects and SEO tags)

The most common migration mistake I see is when an old site is taken down as soon as it's redirected. The SEO friendly approach is to keep the old site and the new site running in parallel after performing the redirect.

Tag the new site page properly to avoid penalization

It is important to have all your pages canonicalized to the new site before you redirect to avoid any duplicate content.

Perform an audit of the new site and fix any broken links, loops, or missing URLs

Check your Google Search Console and Bing Web Master tools. This will allow you to discover crawl errors, mobile usability, pages indexed, top keywords driving traffic and organic search traffic.

New sitemap, new robots, and new site submission for indexing

Submit the new sitemap and robots.txt file to search engines, and keep an eye out for any errors, broken links, and redirects.

Check redirects

As a final check of the new site, check all redirects to ensure there are no redirect loops or inconsistencies.

Also, ensure that all the redirects are 301 redirects. The 301 status code means that a page has permanently moved to a new location.

Site migration might be a bit of a tedious process, but it is crucial that is done correctly. As it is often done once every couple of years, it is best to pay extreme attention to the details throughout this process. If you are not vigilant in the process, you can suffer a loss in visitors or SEO strength that might take a much longer time to bring back.

Sources:
- https://moz.com/blog/web-site-migration-guide-tips-for-seos
- http://searchengineland.com/seo-strategy-during-website-redesign-or-migration-221339

Takeaway

It is absolutely possible to have a successful site migration with little-to-know impact on search rankings. But it means doing the work before, during and after the migration, leaving no stone unturned, and keeping both SEO and user experience in mind, every step of the way. If you are using an outside contractor or agency to handle the migration for you, don't assume they will take SEO into account. Have the discussion beforehand.

Chapter 14

SEO & Code

Most tools used to audit a site don't audit every attribute of the site. That being said, at the end of the day the most important part of SEO is to leave no stone unturned and to capitalize on every opportunity and insight available to ensure your site code is up to par, as solid site code is a critical element of solid SEO.

There are a few ways to see if site code is hindering your site's SEO potential.

Solid HTML

The first site code investigation method is to use HTML validator: https://validator.w3.org/

This tool allows you to analyze the code on your site and see where you can improve it.

In other words, it checks the markup validity, highlighting any errors in feeds, CSS styles, Mobile friendly content, broken code or links.

When you put your site URL into the W3 validator tool, you will be presented with a list of errors and warnings. See figure. 11.1

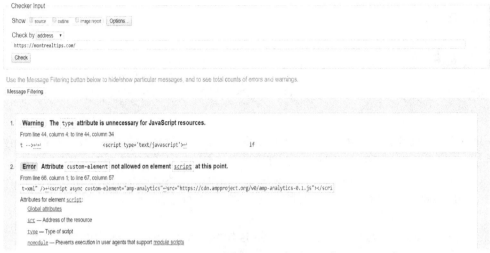

Figure 31.1 – W3 Validator Tools Snapshot Example -
https://validator.w3.org/

Most of the information in this list can be sent to the programmer or developer managing the site. He or she should take the lead on fixing these issues as any changes made without good knowledge of the programming language, the backend, the environment, etc. can have negative impacts on SEO, user experience and more.

Why is fixing these issues important?

Search engine bots and browsers view your site in the same way. They go through the backend of your code and analyze the code and text on the site. As a search engine bot goes through your site, if it finds a lot of errors it will take that as a sign of an ill structured and unmaintained page or overall site. They're looking for useful and accessible. Ill structured and unmaintained don't fit that bill.

Also, these errors can cause a lot of site loading delays or may cause a web page to render improperly. This will cause a bad user experience which is one of the most valued factors when it comes to rankings on SERPs by search engines.

SEO Code to Text Ratio

Another important factor that we have to pay attention to when it comes to SEO and code is the code-to-text ratio.

Although it isn't as important as it was a few years ago, code to text ratio is a good best practice to keep an eye on.

In the past, SEO "experts" tended to add a lot of code to their site vs. actual visual text as a method of tricking search engines. As those engines got smarter, they started looking at this ratio to ensure that whatever was shown to search engines and bots in the code was reflected in the on-page text visible to users. That "expert trick" quickly became useless and most people stopped doing it.

Today, when a search engine or bot encounters a poor code to text ratio, it's usually an indicator of one of two things:
- Whoever is maintaining the site is trying to pull one over on the search engines by showing them one thing and visitors something else.
- The page is not well maintained and has a lot of leftover or messy code that is not serving any purpose.

Neither of these things scream useful or accessible.

So, as much as you might hear talk about this ratio not having a direct impact on site ranking, it definitely does have an indirect impact.

The most common indirect impact is loading delays due to that messy code. Loading delays = poor user experience = unhappy search engines.

Also, this ratio can be an indicator that we have thin content on the page, meaning there is not enough content to provide any real value.

Based on SEMrush research from 2018, the number one pages on Google have 45% more content than the number 20 pages on Google SERPs. A healthy code-to-text ratio does matter. https://www.semrush.com/

How do we check a web page's code-to-text ratio?
To test the code-to-text ratio, check out this tool:
https://smallseotools.com/code-to-text-ratio-checker/

This is a great tool by Small SEO Tools that allows you to get the percentage of code vs text you have on a page.

RESULTS

Page Size	Code Size	Text Size	Code To Text Ratio(%)
75 KB	65 KB	10 KB	13 %

What do these percentages mean?

If the percentage is below 20%, such as the example above, you will need to make some changes.

If the percentage is above 20%, you are in the safe zone. That said, as a best practice, the more text you can add while keeping a page engaging, the better your chances of ranking well.

How can we fix the issue?

What if your ratio is below 20%? What should you be doing? There are 2 ways to fix this.

- Add more content to your site or page. The more text you add, the higher your ratio. Just remember the golden rule of creating for the user first, not the search engines.

- Clean up your code and remove anything that is not being used or is unnecessary.

For me, this is a favourite. Nothing beats looking at the actual code yourself and understanding the process of how the site loads.

To see the code of your page, all you have to do is right click, then click "view page source".

When you see the code, it might be overwhelming at first. But, if you know what you're looking for, you should be fine.

For me, I always look for unnecessary JavaScript.

Here's what to do:

Go to Google Speed Text/Google Page Insights

⚠ Ensure text remains visible during webfont load ⌄

⚠ Minimize main-thread work — 6.4 s ⌄

▦ Reduce JavaScript execution time — 3.5 s ⌄

▦ Serve static assets with an efficient cache policy — 36 resources found ⌄

⬤ Minimize Critical Requests Depth — 10 chains found ⌄

⬤ Keep request counts low and transfer sizes small — 83 requests · 1,455 KB ⌄

If you see that there are notifications with regards to JavaScript, that is usually an opportunity to cleanup some code.

For example, if you go to a site and see JavaScript code for a Facebook pixel, more for a LinkedIn Pixel, more for Google Analytics, then Crazy Egg, Google Search Console, Bing Ads, Bing Web Master Tools…

Instead of leaving all this code floating like that, I recommend creating a GTM account and adding all the tags in there, while only installing the GTM tag on the site. This way, you have code for just one tag instead of several. Depending on the number of tags on a site or page, this can potentially have a significant impact on the code-to-text ratio.

To set up Google Tag Manager see the section below.

-- -- -- -- -- -- -- -- -- -- -- -- -- -- -- -- --

Google Tag Manager
Using GTM to add Google Analytics to your site

GTM stands for Google Tag Manager.

As the name implies, this is a tool for managing the tags on your site. What are web tags? They are pieces of code used to collect information from a web property. One type of tag is a web tag, which can also be called a tracking pixel or analytics tag. One example of a web tag is the little snippet of GA code you get when setting up a Google Analytics account. This tag needs to be implemented across all pages of your site for you to get the most out of Analytics.

Google Tag Manager is also known as a tag container. Like a physical container, it holds multiple things. In this case, multiple tags, from multiple channels. For this section, we'll look at setting up GTM for GA (Google Analytics), but you can use GTM as a tag container for many, many types of tags, thereby reducing the amount of code you have to use on your site or page.

Google Tag Manager also helps us, as marketers and business owners, rely less on developers, as we don't have to enlist the help of developers to add tags to the site. This will avoid major delays since it doesn't have to go into development pipelines and processes.

All we have to do is add the Google Tag Manager snippet to our site once, then we are all set.

GTM Implementation

In this exercise, we will go through the creation of GTM for a site and then connect GA to it.

We'll use the example of The Marketer Within - a theoretical (for now) business with the following URL: https://themarketerwithin.com/

— — — — — — — — — — — — — — — — — — — —

To get started, head to Google Tag Manager:

https://tagmanager.google.com/

Partners   Support

Sign in to Tag Manager   **Start for free**

If you have a Gmail account, you will be prompted to sign in.
If you don't have a Gmail account, get one, then sign in. When you sign in, you will be prompted to create a GTM account.

Q   CREATE ACCOUNT

When you click "Create Account", you will be prompted with an "Add a New Account" window. Fill in the account name and country, and hit continue.

Add a New Account

1 Setup Account

Account Name

The Marketer WIthin

Country

Canada   ▼

☑ Share data anonymously with Google and others

CONTINUE

2 Setup Container

Container Name
Where to Use Container

CREATE   CANCEL

Then enter your container name.

Typically, you use the URL of your site without the https:// part. In this example, that would be "themarketerwithin.com".

Next, select "Web" under "Where to Use Container."

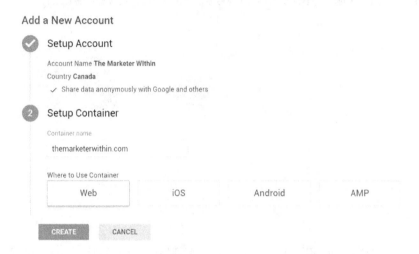

You will then be prompted to add the Google Tag Manager code to your site.

Note that the code must be added in two different places within your site code. Paste the first box of code as high in the <HEAD> section of the site code as possible. Place the second box of code immediately after the <BODY> tag in your site code. As mentioned earlier, clean code is important. If you don't feel totally comfortable doing this, get help.

After you press "OK", you will arrive at the Google Tag Manager dashboard.

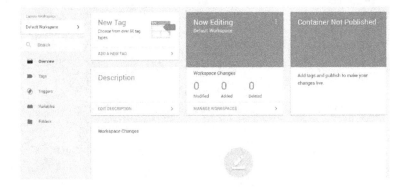

For the sake of this example, we will create a tag that automatically triggers at all the pages on the site. That means, you only have to do this once, and every page within your site will automatically have the tag embedded, even new pages you create down the road. Why would you want this? In this example, we're adding Google Analytics code. Analytics is a tool for tracking all activity on your site, and you typically want that insight across all pages. Having the tracking code added automatically through GTM means less chance of oversight due to human error, and less work for you.

Next, click on "Tags" and "Create New" to create a new tag.

Now name your tag. A great name is "GA Tracking Tag." Our aim here is clarity. No need to get fancy with your naming. You want to be able to come in here and know what something is right away.

Next, click "Tag Configuration." Choose a tag type to begin setup.

As you can see, a window appears prompting you to choose your tag. If you scroll down, you'll see that you can add different types of tags to GTM. They don't have to only be Google-related tags.

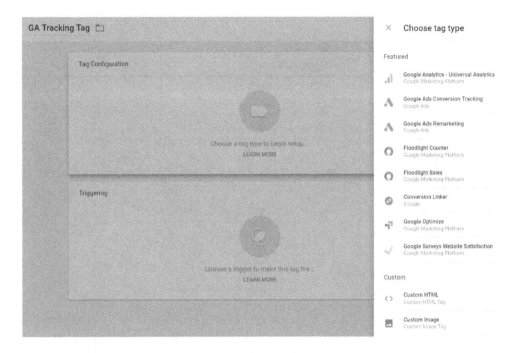

Click on "Google Analytics – Universal Analytics".
Under the "Google Analytics Settings" menu choose "Select New Variable."

This will prompt you to add GA settings, which is where you copy the account number that was generated for you back in Google Analytics. Paste that number under "Tracking ID."

This tracking ID can be found above the tracking code that was given to you by Google when you created your GA account. See the image below:

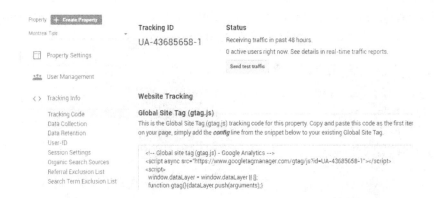

After you paste that code, name your variable - I named mine GA - then click "Save".

After saving, you'll be sent back to the tag page. You'll see that your tag is all set, but you still have to choose where you want it to trigger.

Creating Trigger

In GTM, "Trigger" means on what occasion you want a certain tag to fire.

When you click on "Triggering" (choosing a trigger to make this tag fire), you will be brought to a window like this:

If you want your whole website to be tracked (which is what we want in this example, and what is typically the case for most websites), you will select "All Pages". You'll then be sent back to the previous page with an overview of the confirmation of both the trigger and the tag.

Press save and your tag, variable and trigger will be ready.

Publish

"Publish" means to put it live - into action. Now that you have your tag, variable and trigger, you are ready to publish.

Once you're back at the main dashboard, click "Submit."

You will be led to add a description, which I do recommend adding as it will help you keep track of changes in the future, or across your team. Then click "Publish."

You now officially have GTM added to your site, with GA up and running through an embedded tag. Congrats! From here, you can start using GTM for all your tags to reduce the amount of code on your site and improve your code-to-text ratio. Again, it's really important that your code is clean. It's also really important that everything functions well, so that you can provide the best user experience possible. Setting up GTM is not complicated, but if it feels out of your depth, seek out an expert.

Important Note:

If you already have GA or other tags on your site and have decided to switch to GTM to reduce your code clutter, make sure to first remove the previous tag code from your site.

If you don't, from a GA perspective you will be tracking duplicate content and skewing your data. You'll also just be adding MORE code, when our aim is LESS.

Takeaway

Content may be king, but code matters too. Leave no stone unturned!

Chapter 15

Key SEO/Analytics Measurement Terms

GA Related Terms

GA Important Terms

As mentioned in the previous chapter, Google Analytics is a tool for measuring all activity on your site or web property. If you're working on the SEO of your site, what's something really important to know? If your efforts are having an impact, of course!

Google Analytics is full of useful data and insights that can be used to optimize your overall marketing and business strategies, including your SEO efforts. I highly recommend getting set up with GA before starting on your SEO work, as it will give you a more complete picture of how your site is performing from a search perspective. It can show you:

- How much traffic you're getting from search
- Which search terms are sending traffic your way
- Which of your pages perform best from a search perspective
  - Which ones get the most clicks, drive the most conversions, have the highest user engagement, etc.
- Your overall search performance, not just from a ranking perspective, but in terms of conversions
- What people are doing on your site after they click on a search result

This is critical information as it tells you what's currently working, what isn't, what needs to be improved, and where you have opportunities to optimize and capitalize.

Getting set up with GA before implementing your SEO strategy allows you to get this insight, and establish a baseline, so that you can actually see the impacts your SEO efforts are having.

Once you're set up, the next step is to understand GA better so that you can transform it into relevant insight for your business.

This is the part of Google Analytics that I call "the practice". It's getting you familiar with the tool so that you can get the most benefit from it. An important part of the practice is getting familiar with the important terms: the critical metrics and dimensions that you should learn before you are able to read the actual data on GA reports.

The goal with GA is to translate data into actionable insights. To do that, you need to understand what you're looking at. Here are the key terms and what they mean:

- **Users** = Visitors. These are the total number of people arriving on your site or page during a specified time period.

- **New Users** = New visitors. These are your site or page visitors who have never visited your site before.

- **Sessions** = Visits. Each visit is a new session. If someone arrives on your site, checks out a few pages, then closes their browser window or otherwise leaves your site, that is one session. If they open your site again, that's the beginning of a new session.

- **Returning Users** = Users – New users. These are people who have visited your site before and are now coming back.

- **Pages/Visit (Session)** = The average number of pages viewed by people after hitting a particular landing page.

- **Average Visit (Session) Duration** = The average total time spent on the website during a session.

- **Bounce Rate** = The percentage of visitors that viewed only this page, then left your site without doing anything else.

Dimension	Metrics					
Default Channel Grouping	Acquisition			Behavior		
	Users ↓	New Users	Sessions	Bounce Rate	Pages / Session	Avg. Session Duration
	3,842 % of Total: 100.00% (3,842)	3,773 % of Total: 100.05% (5,771)	4,455 % of Total: 100.00% (4,455)	82.69% Avg for View: 82.69% (0.00%)	1.33 Avg for View: 1.33 (0.00%)	00:01:05 Avg for View: 00:01:05 (0.00%)
1. Organic Search	2,588 (66.72%)	2,558 (67.80%)	2,855 (64.09%)	83.75%	1.29	00:01:01
2. Social	626 (16.14%)	576 (15.27%)	780 (17.51%)	83.72%	1.36	00:00:59
3. Direct	447 (11.52%)	442 (11.71%)	504 (11.31%)	81.75%	1.34	00:00:54
4. Referral	206 (5.31%)	188 (4.98%)	303 (6.80%)	72.61%	1.59	00:02:17
5. Email	10 (0.26%)	8 (0.21%)	10 (0.22%)	60.00%	1.90	00:01:07

The above graphic shows what a typical GA report looks like. The terms we just covered will help you understand it.

— — — — — — — — — — — — — — — — — — —

Metrics in this table are there to describe dimensions.

A dimension can be a traffic source (like search, social media, paid ads, newsletters, etc), or a language (the language of your visitors - note that Google doesn't actually know someone's spoken language, but it can know the language setting on their browser), or any other attribute of your site performance.

Looking at the metrics of a dimension gives you valuable insight into your site performance. For example, it can tell you which traffic sources give you the most engaged, high converting visitors, and where you might need to improve (or even cease efforts). You may know that an overall campaign performed well, but drilling down dimensions in GA can tell you which elements performed best. You may find you're getting significant traffic in a particular language, but visitors are bouncing because your site isn't optimized for multiple languages. This insight can be incredibly valuable and help you concentrate your resources where they will have the most impact.

From an SEO perspective, looking at your search traffic is obviously important, but looking at overall usage matters too. Always remember useful and accessible. Whenever you can improve the user experience on your site, you're impacting your SEO in a positive way. It may not be a direct impact, but when it comes to SEO, indirect impacts can drive significant results.

How is GA divided?

- Audience: Who is visiting your site
- Acquisition: How visitors arrive on your website
- Behaviour: How visitors interact with your website
- Conversions: How visitors complete (or do not complete) conversions on your site

Because every business is unique with unique needs and objectives, GA provides a huge range of data collection and reporting options. Once you're more comfortable with GA, you'll be able to more easily sift through the options and identify those most valuable to you.

As GA is so extensive, it would take thousands of pages and many hours of your time to go over everything. For the sake of this book, we'll keep it to the most essential elements to get you started on tracking your search performance and improving your overall onsite user experience.

Takeaway

Like any digital marketing effort, being able to track your progress is a critical part of SEO. The ideal time to start tracking is before you start implementing your strategy. This gives you a baseline to track progress against, and shows you the areas with the most need and potential for optimization.

Exercise:

Google knows the importance of practice. They also know you don't necessarily want to practice on "the real thing". That's why they've created a demo account specifically for people new to GA to get familiar with the tool. So let's practice!

Go to the Google Analytics Demo Account:

https://analytics.google.com/analytics/web/demoAccount

Navigate through the metrics and get familiar. Remember the terms from the beginning of this chapter. Once you're feeling comfortable with the reports and the terms, get yourself (and your site) set up with GA. This is another setup, like GTM, that really isn't that complex, but if you just don't feel comfortable doing it yourself, get an expert. The same person should be able to do your GTM and GA setup together.

Chapter 16

Common SEO Mistakes

A Look at Some of the Most Common SEO Mistakes

Make Sure Search Engines Can Find You

Sounds simple enough, right? Unfortunately, there are small mistakes you could unknowingly be making that make it impossible for search engines to find your website. And if Google can't find you, neither can your customers.

Make sure you aren't making the following 3 classic SEO mistakes. Verifying and fixing them may require some technical knowledge, but they are quick fixes, so if you do need to bring in outside help, the cost should be quite low.

Mistake #1 - Forgetting to make a site crawlable or indexable

Any effort you put into SEO will be for nothing if search engines are unable to index or crawl your site.

Here are 3 ways to check that you aren't making this mistake:

Make sure robots.txt is not blocking your site

What's robots.txt? This is a file that tells search engines where to enter your site, how to enter, and where not to enter. It's your site's gatekeeper. Search engines know to look for this file.

The easiest way to check your robots.txt file is to type your domain name into the address bar, followed by "/robots.txt".

Example: http://www.exampleyourdomain.com/robots.txt

There should be some text content displayed on the page. If you see nothing but a blank page, no page, or an unattended to page, contact your SEO specialist to update it, immediately.

The robots.txt file is good for both indexing good content, and de-indexing harmful content. If properly used, you will rank for the right pages. If misused, your site could be completely removed from search results. Not good!

Make sure the robots meta tag is set to index

There is a meta tag that could be added to your site head section that tells search engines whether or not to index your site. Setting it to "INDEX" is like putting out a welcome mat. Setting it to "NOINDEX" is like telling the search engines to get off your lawn. Make sure yours is set to "INDEX".

Make sure you have submitted your site and sitemap to Google and Bing

Google and Bing have tools called Google Web Master tools and Bing Web Master tools, respectively. These tools will notify you if there is ever a problem indexing or crawling your site.

- -

Mistake #2 - Duplicate content

When you think about duplicate content, you may think about copying and pasting from another site to your own website. That's not a great practice, but it's not what we're talking about here. We're talking about duplicating your own content.

Here are 3 common scenarios of duplicate content:

Multiple homepages

This when you have 2 or more variations of your home page URL:

www.sample-your-domain.com

www.sample-your-domain.com/index.html
www.sample-your-domain.com/home
www.sample-your-domain.com/default

You would have the exact same content on all these different URLs, but search engines would see each one as a unique page. This dilutes the strength of your homepage so that instead of one homepage getting all the search love, you've got 2, 3 or 4 pages sharing the love. Your homepage is meant to be monogamous.

How to fix it:

Step 1: Choose the one URL you want for your homepage and create 301 redirects from the other URLs that lead to it. The preferable choice is the simplest: www.sample-your-domain.com

Why can't you just delete the other pages? Because the search engines have already indexed them. If you delete them, all that love is gone! Redirecting them sends some of that built up goodness to your main page.

Step 2: Create a canonical tag on your chosen homepage telling search engines to consider that one the homepage.

www. Vs. Non-www.

This is one of the most common mistakes. Having www. and non-www. sites is like splitting all your hard work in half.

Example:
sample-your-domain.com
www.sample-your-domain.com

If both versions of your site exist and are indexable, it's the same as having two websites and the search engine attention gets split. You have to tell Google which one to go to.

How to fix it:
In Google Web Master tools, simply provide Google with your preference. You can choose either the www. or non-www. version of your site. Neither

one is better than the other, but it is critical to choose only one.

Slashes
For example:
www.sample-your-domain.com/services
www.sample-your-domain.com/services/

Once again, search engines will see two separate pages with identical content.

How to fix it:
Add a canonical tag identifying your page preference to ensure search engines only index one of the pages.

- -

Mistake #3 - Ignoring the details

There are a lot of minor details that, if left unchecked, can add up to big problems. Most are easy to fix and cost nothing but a bit of time.

Here are the most commonly ignored details you should check out:

Meta Description: Back in the day, the meta description had a direct impact on SEO. It no longer does, so many people (even specialists) ignore it. Big mistake! There is still an indirect, but significant, impact. It is one of the main influences on click-through-rate (CTR)! Optimizing for CTR must be part of your SEO strategy.

Keyword Location: Important keywords should always be in the first paragraph of your page. Remember our keyword map from earlier? Your primary and secondary keywords should ideally be in the first paragraph (or first and second, if you have very short paragraphs) of your page content. Just remember that user experience is equally - if not more - important. Be sure the keywords make sense where they are.

Page Speed - Clean Code - Clean Site - No HTML Errors: All of these affect the user experience and how browsers and search engines read your site. Google can provide you with page speed insight to help you understand where to improve your site performance and speed.

Also try HTML W3 validator, which was mentioned earlier, to assess your site and identify errors that browsers or search engines might run into. It will show you any errors that might prevent a page from loading fully.

Language Tag: This tag tells search engines the language your page is in and will avoid any duplicate content in cases of similar languages such as UK, Canada and the US, or Mexico, Spain and Chili.

Site Speed: There are two reasons to pay attention to site speed:

1. Making visitors wait even 4-10 seconds will likely lead to a lost conversion.
2. All search engines consider site-speed as a ranking signal.

The PageSpeed Insights tool will tell you what makes your site faster across all devices. You can find the PageSpeed tool here: https://developers.google.com/speed/pagespeed/insights/

Takeaway

If search engines can't find you, or can't figure out how to index you, none of your SEO efforts will have much impact. Take care of the basics.

Chapter 17

Site Structure and SEO

>>

Why Site Structure Matters and What to do About it

Not all websites, pages and blogs are created (or ranked, searched for or indexed) equally. This is true when it's a human interacting with them and when it's a search engine.

If you are a marketer or business owner, you probably know the 80/20 rule of websites: 80% of your business will come from 20% of your pages. If you have a blog of 100 posts, about 20 of those will drive the majority of your conversions (whatever "conversion" means for your business model - it could be a sale, sign up, download, event registration, etc.). This 80/20 breakdown is totally normal and not something that necessarily needs to be "fixed".

However, because a minority of pages drive the majority of conversions, site structure becomes extremely important, for both visitors and search engines.

When I work with a client, one of the first things I do is audit their website to get a clear picture of what we're starting with. Having performed hundreds of such audits, I've come to realize that site structure is a common issue for many businesses.

Think about it like this: brick and mortar stores carefully layout and display merchandise to make it easy for customers to move around and find what they're looking for, and to highlight particular items for quicker sale, or to draw in street traffic.

Site structure is the web equivalent of that practice.

Here are the main disadvantages of not having a well-structured site:

- Dilution of page strength
- Site cannibalization (self-competing)
- Lack of consistency
- Potential for duplicate content
- Harder for search engines to crawl and understand

— — — — — — — — — — — — — — — — — — — —

5 things you can do to get a more structured site:

Divide content into categories.

There are many ways that the human brain and search engines are similar. One of those is that we both LOVE to categorize things! We like it when information fits neatly into set categories. When someone else clearly defines those categories for us (whether human or search engine), we can find things more quickly.

Aggregate related content and organize it into categories or with tags. When you have a lot of content, it is ideal to create a new directory (subdirectory, NOT subdomain as a new subdomain is much harder to rank for). The content in your subdirectories should be specific and should not overlap with other content.

As you categorize and tag your site, ensure that highly related content is put in the right subdirectory as one of your main goals is to avoid cannibalization.

Create a sitemap and submit it to search engines.

XML sitemaps are important for your ranking on SERPs (search engine results pages) because they make it easier for search engines to find pages on your site. Rather than have to follow a bunch of links, search engines know to look for your XML file so they can see all the pages in one place. Kind of like those giant maps in shopping malls.

Another key role of the XML sitemap is to tell search engines which pages are ok to crawl. This way, they know right away which pages not to bother with and can quickly crawl the others.

When creating your sitemap, it's important to know which pages are your key pages, as you will need to organize the map accordingly.

Here is a great tool for creating an effective sitemap: https://www.xml-sitemaps.com/

Once you have your sitemap, add it under your default sitemap URL. That URL should look something like this: https://thecaminowithin.com/sitemap.xml - your website with the /sitemap.xml extension. Use this URL (obviously with your own website, not mine) as your sitemap URL when connecting Google Search Console or Bing Webmaster Tools.

Use canonical tags.

This is one of the most basic and impactful optimization tools. It's a way of telling search engines that a certain page represents the original copy of a page in order to avoid duplicate content.

We touched on this concept a bit earlier. The word "canon" means, generally, "authoritative". When a page is canonical, it means that's the main one. The original. It's the one that should be referenced above all others like it. So, if you have different URLs hosting the same content, designate one page as "canon" to instruct search engines to ignore the others. This ensures all search strength is directed towards your one main page, and not diluted among many.

Here's an example of a canonical page: https://thecaminowithin.com. That's my canonical homepage, but all these URL structures may be considered variations of that page:

https://thecaminowithin.com/
http://thecaminowithin.com/
https://www.thecaminowithin.com/

To the human eye, we can tell that these are probably all the same page. But, without canonical tags, a search engine will see all these as separate.

Use a tag like this to tell search engines which page is your canon page: <link rel="Canonical" href="https://thecaminowithin.com">

Remove duplicate pages, content or tags.

Duplicate content happens when content appears in more than one place within the same website. It makes your site repetitive and irrelevant for both humans and search engines.

When navigating through a website, both humans and search engines look for (and expect) unique information or content with each new page visit. Duplicate content makes it hard to figure out what is original and what is not. It confuses search engines in deciding which version should get ranking strength and which should be ignored.

The best analogy is that you are taking a good piece of content and watering it down. Diluting its strength.

Aim for all your content to be unique, concentrating on the following areas:
1. Duplicate titles and descriptions.
2. Duplicate headers.
3. Duplicate paragraphs.

Interlink properly.

An internal link is a type of hyperlink on a webpage that links to another resource (page, image, document, etc) within the same site.

There are many advantages to interlinking, such as connecting relevant pages, enabling visitors to easily find information and helping them spend more time on your site.

But, when it comes to interlinks, you must stay structured, relevant, consistent and not overdo it. A best practice is to use relevant and descriptive anchor text that relates to the content of the page or resource you are linking to.

Just like a brick and mortar business, your website needs to be well structured for it to perform optimally. Don't ignore site structure. Master it.

References:

- https://yoast.com/site-structure-the-ultimate-guide/#why-important
- https://moz.com/learn/seo/internal-link

Takeaway

Site structure is key to accessibility and usefulness, and matters for both humans and search engines.

Chapter 18

SEO Audits: Easy SEO Audit Guide

How to Do a Basic DIY Site Audit Without Fancy Tools

Nobody likes an audit. Any kind of audit! And, when it comes to an SEO audit, digital marketing specialists have a tendency to overcomplicate things.

The truth is, most of the big-ticket items impacting your SEO are things you can easily look into on your own to see where you stand and what you need to do to bring your site up to par. You do need to know your metadata from your messaging, but you don't need to be a digital ninja/guru/magician to do a basic audit.

Here are the 6 most important factors to look at in your <u>basic</u> SEO audit.

---

1. Page Titles, Descriptions, & URLs

I said it would be easy. I didn't say it wouldn't be a bit tedious! Yes, you need to look at these things for every page you are intending to audit.

The page titles, descriptions and URLs are what appear in Google, Bing or other search engine results pages.

Title

- Is it between 40 to 70 characters?
- Is it informative - does it adequately describe what the business does or the content of that page?
- Does it include the keywords you want to rank for?

Description

- Is it between 120-155 characters?
- Is it informative?
- Does it include the keywords you want to rank for?
- Does it intrigue the searcher to click on your search result?

URL

- Is it HTTPs? HTTPs is preferred over HTTP across the whole site.
- Is it informative?
- Are all characters in lowercase?
- Are you using hyphens instead of underscores? Remember, underscores read as nothing whereas hyphens read as spaces - use hyphens.
- Is it free of any non-ASCII characters?
- Are all URLs across the site free of inconsistent parameters?

---

2. Content Quality

Keywords are a start. But there's more to quality SEO content than hitting the right keywords. Relevancy, consistency and value to the reader are all critical elements of good SEO content as well. When auditing your content, look for the following quality factors:

- Is there a consistent use of keywords across the site and in tags?
- Is there a good keyword density?
- Does the keyword strategy follow a proper keyword map to avoid competing pages?
- Is there both dynamic and static content?
- Is the content relevant to the industry/product/service?
- Is the content share-worthy?
- Does the content drive value to the reader?
- Are you targeting a select number of keywords vs. keyword stuffing?

- -

3. Content Quantity & Diversity

The amount of unique content on your site is also a factor.

- Is there a good amount of text on each page?
- Is there a good code-to-text ratio?
- Is there diversity in which content is shown?
- Are you capitalizing on text, PDF, video, images, slides, etc?

---

4. Site Structure and Index-ability

We're moving into more technical territory, but everything here is fairly simple to look into without any fancy tools.

- Are the pages, posts, and properties mapped properly?
- Is there a clean and up-to-date sitemap?
- It there a proper interlinking approach implemented on site? (i.e. linking to other pages, and posts within your site.)
- Are you using your robots.txt file properly? As mentioned earlier, check by typing www.yourdomain.com/robots.txt into your address bar. This file will show you if you are accidentally de-indexing your site.
- Is the site free of broken links? Broken links are a sign that your site may need technical optimization.

---

5. Page Speed and Functionality

- Does each page load quickly? To see if something is slowing down your site, use the Google Page Insight test here: https://developers.google.com/speed/pagespeed/insights/
- Is the site free of broken links?
- Is everything on the site loading properly? (images, videos, forms, menus, etc.)
- Is the site mobile friendly? To check, try Google's Mobile Friendly test here: https://search.google.com/search-console/mobile-friendly

---

6. User Experience

Last, but not least, ensure your site is easy to use.

- Is the site easy to navigate? (You are probably very familiar with your own site, so it's a good idea to ask people who aren't to go through it and see if they have any trouble navigating the content.)
- Is there proper internal linking?

- Is there a call to action and/or a clear message on the site?
- Can visitors easily and quickly understand what your business is about?
- Do you have the most important elements on your site above the fold?

Takeaway:

You don't necessarily need a specialist or a set of pro-tools to audit your site. All you need is some attention to detail, a little time and to know where to look. The time you invest in your audit and any optimizations based on your findings will pay off, big time. If you are intending to take things to the next level, and feel out of your depth, then consider hiring an SEO expert.

Chapter 19

4 Free Tools to Audit Site Performance

4 Free Tools to Track Website Performance

When you have a site or blog that has been running for years, and you start to see numbers dropping, visitors not returning, conversions decreasing...

The question becomes, why?

In situations like this, what's affecting site performance usually can't be summed up in one easy answer. As a marketer, businessperson, or entrepreneur, you should be keeping an eye on many factors, but there are some key areas of focus to pay special attention to.

The main factors that have been impacting site performance over the past few years, and the questions you should ask yourself are:

1. Is my site mobile friendly? How do I find out and what should I fix?
2. Is my site's speed optimal? How can I make it faster?
3. Is my site ranking well on search engines? How can I test this?
4. Does my site contain coding errors? How can I fix them? Are search engines and browsers reading my site properly? Is my site compatible?

Let's explore each of these questions and their answers:

1. Is my site mobile friendly? How do I find out and what should I fix?

Answer:
Put away your smartphone because Google has an amazing tool called Google Mobile-Friendly Test Tool that will give you the answer to that first question.

Google's Mobile-Friendly Test Tool is a quick-and-easy way to see how people see your site when accessing it from a mobile device. To optimize mobile performance, look at how your site renders on mobile devices and ask yourself these four simple questions:

1. Is the text on the site too small to read?
2. Is the content on the site wider than the screen?
3. Is the mobile viewport set? (this is a meta-tag telling browsers to adapt to the proper screen size)
4. Are links too close together making them difficult to tap? i.e. Is your site harder to navigate on mobile?

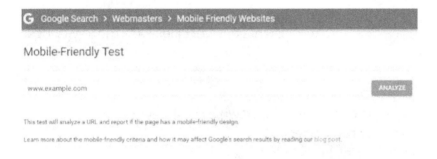

You can find the Mobile-Friendly Test Tool here: https://www.google.com/webmasters/tools/mobile-friendly/

2. Is my site's speed optimal? How can I make it faster?

Answer:
There's a rather simple solution to the problems posed by both questions here: the PageSpeed Insights tool.

What is exceptional about the PageSpeed Insights tool is that it tells you what makes your site faster across all devices, so you don't just get clarity on your site's speed, you also get solutions if your site speed isn't up to par.

Why is site speed important? Well, seeing that our collective attention span is getting shorter and shorter, making visitors wait anywhere between 4-10 seconds will likely lead to a lost conversion. And, let's not forget that all search engines consider site speed as a ranking signal.

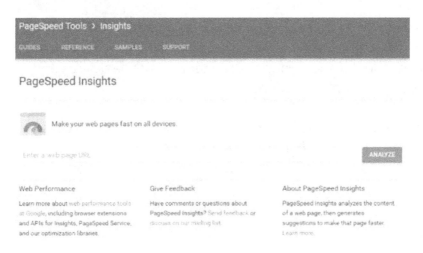

So, what questions can PageSpeed Insights answer? Here are the key things to look for:

- Are you using legible font sizes?
- Is the page too big or too small for the viewport? (Mobile)
- Is your viewport configured correctly?
- Do you have any Javascript of CSS blocking any above-the-fold content?
- Are your images configured for optimal performance?
- Is your server response time optimal?
- Are you leveraging browser caching?
- Are you misusing landing page redirects?

You can find the tool here:
https://developers.google.com/speed/pagespeed/insights/

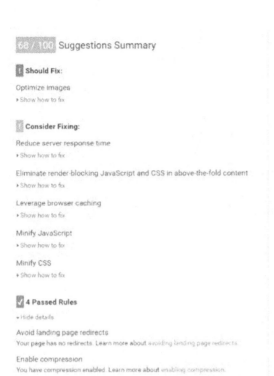

3. Is my site ranking well on search engines? How can I test this?

Answer:
One of the most useful tools that many marketers aren't capitalizing on is the Google search tool, meaning the search engine itself.

As obvious as it sounds, using Google can provide you with tons of details on how your site is ranking.

That being said, there is a not-quite-as-obvious way to use Google when tracking your site's performance.

The best way to see if your site is being indexed is by just adding "site:" before your site's URL. Google will then return the search results within the specific URL, and if your site doesn't show up in the results, it means your site is not indexed.

What you type into Google's search bar would look something like this: "Site: example.com"

You can find the tool here: https://www.google.com

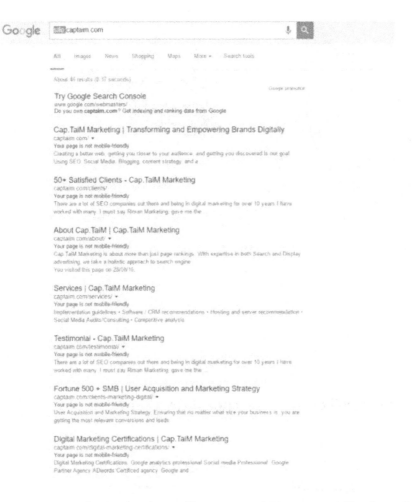

4. Does my site contain coding errors? How can I fix them? Are search engines and browsers reading my site properly? Is my site compatible?

Answer:
Owning a site that contains absolutely no coding errors is quite rare. If anything, it's more normal that a site has coding errors. You see, after many updates and changes, errors can begin piling up, entirely unbeknownst to you. And the more this happens the harder it gets for search engine bots or browsers to go through your page.

This might cause a lot of problems, such as:

1. The site will not get indexed properly
2. The site will not load properly
3. The site will stop showing properly

4. Some pieces of important code (such as Google Analytics, if placed at the bottom of the page) will not load properly and not record visits or conversions.
5. The site will be slower.

All in all, it is important to test your site constantly and fix any issues immediately.

My advice is to test your site. A great tool to test is the W3C Validation Service. Print the page in PDF and send it to your programmer to get the problems sorted.

You can find the W3C Validation Service here: https://validator.w3.org/

How can you take action?

Don't wait another minute and have users be frustrated by your site's poor performance. My advice is to check your site across all these tools right away, print the results, and send them to your marketer, programmer, and SEO expert. Ensure everything is handled right away and enjoy a site that has reached a new level of optimized performance.

Takeaway

As time goes on, your website will change and evolve, algorithms will change and evolve, and the technology people use to access your site will change and evolve. All of this can impact your site performance and, therefore, your rankings. If your rankings start to drop, look into your site performance.

Chapter 20

SEO & Entrepreneurship

The Modern SEO Guide for Entrepreneurs

How often do we hear that SEO is dead, obsolete, or not as important as it was a few years ago?

The Search Engine Marketing industry is in constant change. There are continuous updates and algorithm changes across all search engines every couple of months and, in some instances, each day. That makes it seem like more of a challenge to keep up, and small business owners and entrepreneurs can easily get overwhelmed.

But the challenge does not make the practice obsolete.

The use of search engines to find products and services has certainly not decreased. It has increased. Massively. As long as people continue to use search engines, optimizing to rank well will continue to be a solid and smart investment. Remember, wherever your audience is, that's where you want to be.

Over the past 7 years, I have worked with SEO for agencies, Fortune 500s and small businesses. In that time, I've learned that there are some SEO factors that never change.

If you are hesitant about 'keeping up' with the latest in SEO, at the very least ensure you are capitalizing on these 6 constants.

1. Optimizing for humans, not search engines

Is this getting repetitive? That's because it is SO important. If you remember nothing else from this book, remember that the human comes first.

Although "SEO" stands for Search Engine Optimization, the optimization you do truly is more for humans than search engines. After all, the people are your customers. Not the engines.

To rank well, think about the human experience rather than the search engines. **Focus on human engagement**, relevancy to searchers, what will be most attractive to people, rather than stuffing in keywords just to appeal to search engines.

2. Focusing on what makes you different

What makes you different from anyone else offering a similar product or service? Be clear on what makes you different. Ensure you have content on your website and in your SEO strategy that highlights it. Your differentiator is what will stand out and attract attention when someone is doing a search.

I always tell my clients that **SEO is more about you** than it is about technical optimization and upgrades. It is about showing your business, service, product, values and unique selling point with the right content while tapping into the searcher's intent. To do that, ask yourself, "What is my target audience thinking when they are searching for my specific product or service?" Your answer will often tell you what to highlight.

3. User experience

Always look at your own site from a visitor's perspective.

People spend more time on sites that are easy to navigate, drive value and educate them. More time on site increases the chances of conversions (i.e. more clients/customers). Search engines also look at time on site as an important ranking factor, as it is an indicator that you are useful and accessible to users.

As long as there are users, user experience will never go out of style. Make sure your site is responsive and fast to load, creating a seamless user experience.

4. Clean site structure

Clean and organized goes a long way, especially in search engines. You can know a lot about a site just by looking at the URL. Any unconventional characters, a mix of upper- and lower-case characters, parameters, and excessive categories and sub-directories all make for a messy site structure. Have a structured site and clean URLs. This makes it easier for search engines to navigate your site and index your pages.

5. Abiding by the rules

Search engines are smarter than we think they are. Whatever trick you are thinking of pulling on Google... trust me, Google has seen it before.

Remember what we reviewed earlier about black hat SEO tactics. More often than not, they'll end up getting your site penalized by search engines. And that is hard to recover from.

Also, most black hat tactics provide little value to your audience and don't drive conversions. When it comes to driving traffic, you want quality traffic that converts and helps your business grow. I'll say it again: focus on the user.

Creating value and driving traffic through hard work is rewarding and effective.

Don't put yourself in a bad situation or at risk of getting penalized for petty rankings.

6. Creating great content and driving value

Content is king! Ten years ago, marketers and SEO specialists lived by this mantra. And it is still true today. Great content is simply great SEO.

Remember that content is not only text. Content is video, images, slides, whitepapers, pdfs, etc.

When you have a valuable piece of content that will educate, entertain or otherwise engage your audience, share it and tag it properly.

Takeaway

When it comes to investing in SEO, don't hesitate out of a mistaken belief that SEO has little impact, or that what you do today will be obsolete tomorrow. SEO is an integral part of digital marketing. The six factors above don't get a lot of airplay these days, only because they aren't shiny and new. Rather, they are tried and true tactics for ranking well. Use them as a guide for your SEO efforts and the investment into your website will pay for itself many times over.

Chapter 21

SEO and Search Engines

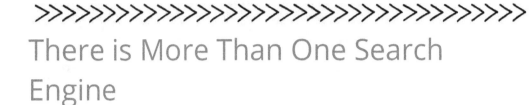

There is More Than One Search
Engine

When we think search, most of us think Google. However, it is still not the only player in the market. Most of the marketing experts that I have met consider SEO to be Google and Google to be SEO, but that's missing out on a non-insignificant market segment.

For the past few years, Google has controlled approximately 70% of the Canadian search market. And, if we look outside Canada and North America, there is often an even greater non-Google audience. 70% may seem high, but that still leaves nearly ⅓ of the market using services other than Google. No good marketer would ever ignore a third of their market.

To ensure we are not ignoring this market, we need to be aware of the other players:

- Bing
- Yahoo
- Yandex
- Baidu
- YouTube
- Amazon

Pretty much any site that includes listings is a search engine, and operates according to similar principles as Google - it is looking to provide the best value and accessibility to its users as possible.

Because Google is the largest and most influential search engine, if you optimize for Google, there's a good chance that work will impact your rankings in other search engines as well. Especially if your approach is to prioritize the user. However, it isn't a given. Don't make the mistake of

196 | **The SEO Way** | Search Engine Optimization for Beginners

ignoring non-Google search engines. Check your rankings, investigate issues, optimize for better results.

Takeaway

Google is big, but it isn't everything. Don't make the mistake of ignoring significant market segments.

Chapter 22

SEO & Google Search Console

When it comes to SEO, the truth is there is no SEO without Google.

Ok, so we just had a short chapter on the importance of not ignoring non-Google search engines. And that really is important, but... Google still is "the big one". There are a lot of great search engines out there, many with strong user bases, but there are currently none as large or as influential as Google.

Google has been in constant improvement mode for the past 20 years. It has been, and continues to be, continuously striving to bring users what they want in the fastest, most accessible ways possible.

Because of this, Google wants marketers and SEO experts to succeed. They want good content and good businesses. Without good results to provide, Google's search engine would cease to exist. And so, Google gives SEO experts and marketers a tool that allows them to manage their search results in the best way possible.

This tool is not designed to help people manipulate results or game the system. It is to help people improve their site content and structure, and ensure they are not running into any issues on Google.

The tool is called Google Search Console. Historically it was known as Google Web Master Tools, but has since been rebranded.

From an SEO perspective, it is critical that you connect your site to Google Search Console.

Here's how:

1. Go to https://search.google.com/search-console/about
2. Click the "Start Now" button, and signup using your Gmail account.
3. You will be forwarded to a page where you can verify your site on Google Search Console.

There are 2 options for doing this:

1. Add a domain (For this you will need to have access to the domain DNS records). This option allows you to include all the subdomains, variations, and protocols that you have on the site.

2. URL prefix. This is currently the most commonly used option at this point. It allows you to add a specific URL, and it allows you a multiple verification method.

For the sake of this example, and assuming that your site has one domain and no subdomains, we'll go through the URL prefix method.

We will go with the example of adding captaim.com (my marketing agency website).

We'll add this site under URL prefix: https://captaim.com/

Once I click "continue", I'll be provided with different verification options. Typically, I choose the "HTML tag" option, as this allows me to add it to the site's header.

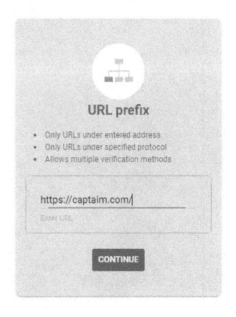

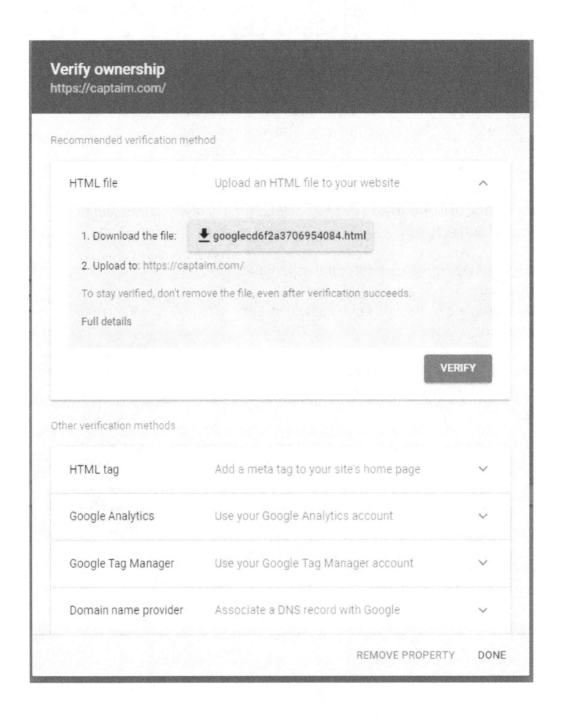

Choosing the HTML tag option, I am provided with a meta tag to add to the head section of my site.

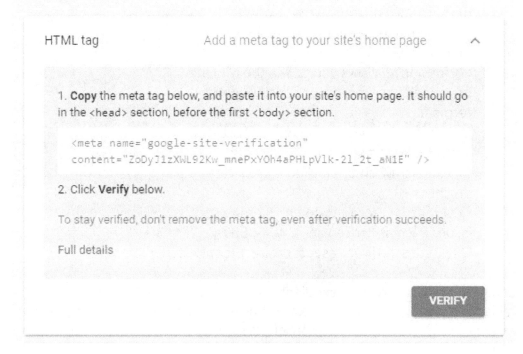

Other verification methods

HTML tag   Add a meta tag to your site's home page   ∧

1. **Copy** the meta tag below, and paste it into your site's home page. It should go in the `<head>` section, before the first `<body>` section.

```
<meta name="google-site-verification"
content="ZoDyJ1zXWL92Kw_mnePxYOh4aPHLpVlk-2l_2t_aN1E" />
```

2. Click **Verify** below.

To stay verified, don't remove the meta tag, even after verification succeeds.

Full details

VERIFY

I go to my site, paste in my tag, and click verify.

Scripts in Header

```
<meta name="google-site-verification"
content="ZoDyJ1zXWL92Kw_mnePxYOh4aPHLpVlk-
2l_2t_aN1E" />
```

These scripts will be printed in the `<code><head></code>` section.

The moment the site is verified by Google Search Console, I am able to view some essential functionalities on Google Search Console.

- Overview allows you to see the performance of your site on Google Search Engine Results Pages as well as a quick overview of coverage.
- Performance allows you to see the ranking of your site and pages for specific search terms.
- URL inspection allows you to inspect URLs individually and see if they are being indexed, crawled or blocked by search engines.
- Coverage is where can see if your site has issues such as broken links, 404s, 500s, URL issues, redirect issues, redirect loops, etc...

Google Search Console is an excellent and extremely powerful tool. Yet, as we know, with great power comes great responsibility. We have to be careful when we are managing a site's search console as small changes can cause huge problems.

Takeaway

Search engines don't exist without anything good to search for. Because of this, search engines like Google *want* you to succeed and create tools to help you do that. Take advantage of this.

Chapter 23

SEO and Bing Web Master Tools

Bing Web Master Tools

SEO as part of the digital ecosystem

As mentioned in the previous chapters, Google is not the only search engine out there and we can't ignore the other players in the game. Next in line to Google is Bing. And so, we will now go through the creation process for Bing Web Master Tools.

To get started, go to Bing Web Master tools:
https://www.bing.com/toolbox/webmaster

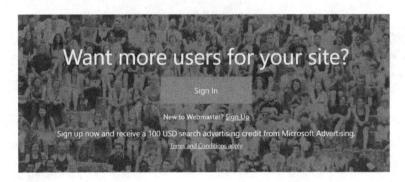

You can choose to log in using one of the email accounts that you own: Microsoft, Google or Facebook.

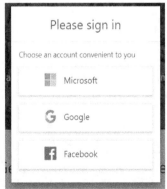

For this example, we'll choose Microsoft.

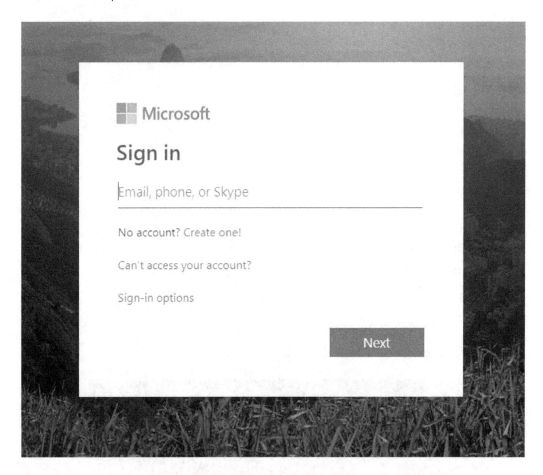

If you don't have a @live, @hotmail or @outlook account, you will need to create one for this sign in option to work (otherwise, you can use Google or Facebook).

Once you're logged in, you will be able to access Bing Web Master tools and will be prompted to add your site.

Once again, I'll be using https://captaim.com for this example. As I add the URL to Bing Web Master Tools site, I am prompted to add the sitemap as well.

We've mentioned sitemaps a few times now, and will cover how to create one in another chapter.

Add a Site

ABOUT MY WEBSITE

URL *

https://captiam.com

Add a sitemap ⓘ

https://captiam.com/sitemap.xml

When do you receive the most traffic to this site for your local time of the day? ⓘ

All Day (Default) ▾

ADD

After clicking "add", I am prompted to verify the site using any of the 3 different options.

Option 1: Place an XML file on your web server
Option 2: Copy and paste a <meta> tag in your default webpage
Option 3: Add CNAME record to DNS

I always choose option 2. Once I add the meta tag to the header of my site, I am quickly provided with access to Bing Web Master Tools.

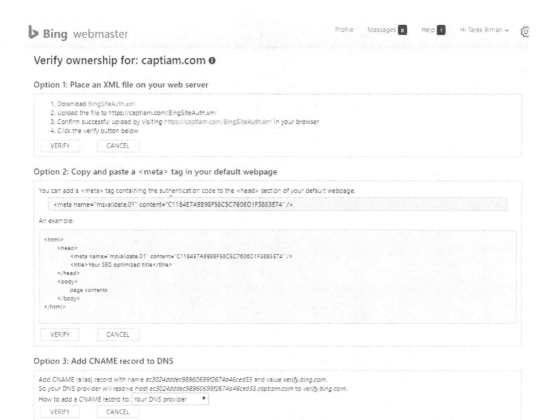

Verify ownership for: captiam.com ⓘ

Option 1: Place an XML file on your web server

1. Download BingSiteAuth.xml
2. Upload the file to https://captiam.com/BingSiteAuth.xml
3. Confirm successful upload by visiting https://captiam.com/BingSiteAuth.xml in your browser
4. Click the verify button below

VERIFY   CANCEL

Option 2: Copy and paste a <meta> tag in your default webpage

You can add a <meta> tag containing the authentication code to the <head> section of your default webpage.

```
<meta name="msvalidate.01" content="C1184E7A9B98F58C5C7606D1F3883E74" />
```

An example:

```
<html>
    <head>
        <meta name="msvalidate.01" content="C1184E7A9B98F58C5C7606D1F3883E74" />
        <title>Your SEO optimized title</title>
    </head>
    <body>
        page contents
    </body>
</html>
```

VERIFY   CANCEL

Option 3: Add CNAME record to DNS

Add CNAME (alias) record with name ec3024dddec98960699f2674a46ced55 and value verify.bing.com.
So your DNS provider will resolve host ec3024dddec98960699f2674a46ced55.captiam.com to verify.bing.com.

How to add a CNAME record to: Your DNS provider ▼

VERIFY   CANCEL

Takeaway

Because Google is currently the biggest and most influential search engine on the market, optimizing for Google will usually optimize for other search engines as well. But don't just take that as a given. Invest some time and effort into the tools available from other search engines, like Bing. It may not be the largest market segment, but it has value.

Chapter 24

The Acquisition Report

>>

SEO as Part of the Digital Ecosystem

Google Analytics Acquisition Report Overview

The acquisition report is an incredibly useful report in Google Analytics that reflects how people are coming to your site. In this chapter, we'll walk through how to read and understand this report. If you haven't setup GA yet, you'll be able to use the Google Demo account to practice.

As a marketer, entrepreneur and business owner, this is one of the main reports that I rely on for my site because it gives me the best picture of where new users are coming from, what they do once they arrive and where I need to concentrate efforts to drive the best ROI possible. Once again, remember useful and accessible. Getting insight into where people are coming from and how they interact with your site empowers you to continually optimize for usefulness and accessibility. Also remember that SEO is holistic. Strong SEO is built by working on all aspects of the big picture, not just search traffic.

Acquisition Overview Report

This report allows you to see the best sources of traffic to your site and how visitors from these specific sources are interacting with your site. In other words, you get insight into what's working and what's relevant.

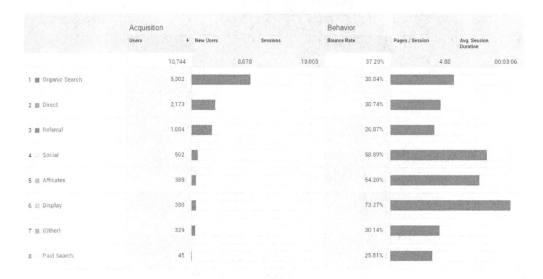

Acquisition All Traffic Report

This report allows you to see, in detail, how traffic from specific channels, sources and mediums is behaving on your site.

As you can see in the report below, we are shown both the behaviour and the acquisition metrics associated with specific sources and mediums.

Source / Medium	Acquisition			Behavior		
	Users ↓	New Users	Sessions	Bounce Rate	Pages / Session	Avg. Session Duration
	10,744 % of Total: 100.00% (10,744)	8,685 % of Total: 100.06% (8,679)	13,063 % of Total: 100.00% (13,063)	37.29% Avg for View 37.29% (0.00%)	4.88 Avg for View: 4.88 (0.00%)	00:03:06 Avg for View: 00:03:06 (0.00%)
1. google / organic	5,145 (46.44%)	4,254 (48.98%)	5,976 (45.75%)	38.20%	4.84	00:02:56
2. (direct) / (none)	2,178 (19.66%)	1,809 (20.83%)	2,657 (20.34%)	30.71%	5.10	00:03:40
3. mail.googleplex.com / referral	1,125 (10.15%)	506 (5.83%)	1,483 (11.35%)	12.27%	7.96	00:04:51
4. analytics.google.com / referral	572 (5.16%)	393 (4.52%)	665 (5.09%)	54.89%	2.61	00:02:33
5. Partners / affiliate	389 (3.51%)	344 (3.96%)	441 (3.38%)	54.20%	3.22	00:02:05
6. dfa / cpm	380 (3.43%)	356 (4.10%)	419 (3.21%)	73.27%	2.10	00:00:58
7. creatoracademy.youtube.com / referral	349 (3.15%)	336 (3.87%)	356 (2.73%)	67.42%	2.24	00:00:46
8. (not set) / (not set)	329 (2.97%)	235 (2.71%)	355 (2.72%)	30.14%	5.42	00:02:52
9. baidu / organic	89 (0.80%)	88 (1.01%)	90 (0.69%)	84.44%	1.56	00:00:26
10. groups.google.com / referral	59 (0.53%)	32 (0.37%)	88 (0.67%)	28.41%	5.31	00:03:56

This is a goldmine for marketers as it can help identify the mediums that work and the mediums that don't. A huge part of GA's value is in its ability to help us see clearly, and on a granular level, what's working and what isn't, so that we can respond accordingly and continually take our businesses and websites to the next level.

Acquisition Referral Report

This report allows you to see, in detail, which websites are linking to yours and the amount of traffic that these sites are sending to yours.

Source	Acquisition			Behavior		
	Users ↓	New Users	Sessions	Bounce Rate	Pages / Session	Avg. Session Duration
	2,439 % of Total: 22.70% (10,744)	1,522 % of Total: 17.54% (8,678)	2,984 % of Total: 22.84% (13,065)	33.45% Avg for View: 37.29% (-10.31%)	5.42 Avg for View: 4.88 (11.14%)	00:03:28 Avg for View: 00:03:06 (11.77%)
1. mall.googleplex.com	1,125 (45.96%)	506 (33.25%)	1,483 (49.70%)	12.27%	7.96	00:04:51
2. analytics.google.com	572 (23.37%)	393 (25.82%)	665 (22.29%)	54.89%	2.61	00:02:33
3. creatoracademy.youtube.com	349 (14.26%)	336 (22.08%)	356 (11.93%)	67.42%	2.24	00:00:46
4. groups.google.com	59 (2.41%)	32 (2.10%)	88 (2.95%)	28.41%	5.31	00:03:56
5. m.facebook.com	57 (2.33%)	56 (3.56%)	59 (1.98%)	67.80%	2.17	00:00:39

This is especially important when working on your site's SEO and on link building as it can be a great reference of site SEO performance, as search engines do take into account the number and quality of external links leading to your site.

It can also help you identify potential partnership or advertising opportunities based on the quality of traffic external sites are sending your way.

Acquisition Google Ads Report

This report allows you to see, in detail, how your Google Ads paid campaigns are performing and how they are yielding results on your site. Under the Google Ads report (previously Google AdWords Report), you can see the performance of the account, campaigns, sitelinks, final URL, display, video, shopping and keywords.

Highlighting all the critical attributes of a Google Ads campaign, this report opens the door to not only understanding what is bringing clicks, but also to understanding what keyword, account, ad or campaign is yielding higher engagement on the site.

To have proper access to this report, you have to link your GA account with your Google Ads account. This is not done by default.

To link them, navigate to the admin panel in GA and, under the property panel, select "Google Ads linking". A list of your AdWords accounts (if you have any) will show up. Check the one that you want to link, click continue and you're all set.

If you don't have an AdWords account and aren't sure if you want or need one, don't worry. We'll explore AdWords a little more later on to help you determine if it's right for your business.

Campaign / Campaign ID		Acquisition					Behavior			Conversions eCommerce ▾		
		Clicks ↓	Cost	CPC	Users	Sessions	Bounce Rate	Pages / Session	Ecommerce Conversion Rate	Transactions	Revenue
		134 % of Total: 100.00% (134)	$60.95 % of Total: 100.00% ($60.95)	$0.45 Avg for View: 33.45 (0.00%)	159 % of Total: 14% (10,744)	178 % of Total: 1.36% (13,073)	40.45% Avg for View: 27.43% (7.50%)	4.14 Avg Fir View: 4.89 (-14.54%)	0.56% Avg for View: 0.72% (-39.20%)	1 % of Total: 8.25% (16)	$399.26 % of Total: 37.27% (31,411.19)
1	AW - Youtube Apparel 769500980		88 (65.67%)	$47.43 (77.82%)	$0.54	79 (49.30%)	80 (44.94%)	63.75%	2.00	0.00%	0 (0.00%)	$0.00 (0.00%)
2	AW - Apparel 15895H429		32 (23.88%)	$9.19 (15.08%)	$0.29	25 (15.40%)	26 (14.61%)	23.00%	6.81	3.85%	1 (100.00%)	$399.26 (100.00%)
3	AW - Google Brand 1695507726		6 (4.48%)	$0.74 (1.21%)	$0.12	5 (3.12%)	6 (3.47%)	0.00%	3.20	0.00%	0 (0.00%)	$0.00 (0.00%)

Acquisition Search Console Report

This report provides you detailed information on the performance of queries, pages, devices and locations in Google organic/natural search results. Organic search is what SEO is all about. It is the unpaid search results that come up on Google or other search engines when someone enters a search term. They are differentiated from the paid results that are often displayed at the top or side of search engine results pages.

Similar to the Google Ads report, you have to set up this link, as it is not provided by default. The message below should appear when you attempt to access this report without the link:

This report requires Search Console integration to be enabled.

Set up Search Console data sharing

What is Search Console?
Search Console is a free product that provides data and analytics to help improve your site's performance in Google search.

Enabling Search Console data within Analytics
Once you connect a site you own in Search Console to your Analytics property, its data becomes visible in your Search Engine Optimization reports. You can visit the Property Settings page in Analytics account management to change which of your Search Console sites' data you wish to show, and control which views on your Web Property have access to view the data.

How to use Search Console data within Analytics
Search Console provides data about what users see in Google search results before they decide to click to your site (or some other site). You can use this data to identify opportunities and prioritize development effort to increase the number of visitors to your site. Examples:

- Identify landing pages on your site that have good clickthrough rates (CTR), but have poor average positions in search results. These could be pages that people want to see, but have trouble finding.
- Identify search queries (keywords) for which your site has good average positions, but poor click through rates. These are queries for which your pages get attention and improved content could lead to more visitors.

Click on "Set up Search Console data sharing" and you will be brought to the property setting page. Scroll down until you see "Search Console":

Search Console

Adjust Search Console

Click "Adjust Search Console" and you will be redirected to a page where you can add the associated Google Search Console property.

Search Console Settings

Search Console site ?
By linking your Analytics property to your Search Console account(s), Search Console data will be imported in Analytics and included in your Google Analytics reporting. Learn more
none   Add

Done

Click "Add" and you will see a full list of your Google Search Console properties.

https://montrealtips.com/   This site is not linked to any web property in your Google Analytics account.
http://www.montrealtips.com/   This site is not linked to any web property in your Google Analytics account.

Click the property that you want to integrate with GA and click "Save". You will then see the following message:

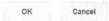

Add association

You are about to save a new association. Any existing Search Console association for this web property will be removed.

OK   Cancel

Press "OK" and you're all set.

To verify that the connection was successful, go to admin panel > property > product linking, then click "All Products." You should see something similar to the following:

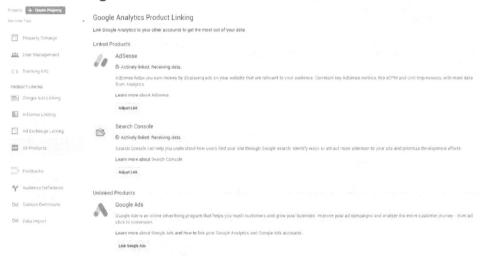

Now that you have access to the Google Search Console data, you can start seeing not only what keywords and pages are bringing the most organic traffic to your site, but also how engaged the visitors on these pages are and whether or not they are converting. As you can imagine, this is hugely beneficial to any SEO efforts.

Acquisition Social Report

The social report allows you to identify your most successful social networks and campaigns in terms of bringing traffic and conversions to your web property.

The report highlights social network performance, your best performing landing pages, conversions driven from social channels, and the user flow for visitors arriving from these social channels.

Social Network	Sessions	% Sessions
1. YouTube	388	60.82%
2. Facebook	118	18.50%
3. Google Groups	80	12.54%
4. Quora	24	3.76%
5. reddit	17	2.66%
6. Pinterest	4	0.63%
7. wikiHow	4	0.63%
8. Twitter	2	0.31%
9. Google+	1	0.16%

It is important to note that GA qualifies YouTube, Facebook, Google Groups, Quora, Reddit, Pinterest, wikiHow, Twitter, Google+, LinkedIn, Blogger, Pocket and VK as examples of social networks.

When it comes to social networks, I find that landing pages tend to be big players, as we often link to specific pages in our efforts and campaigns rather than simply our homepage. As such, I find the greatest value in the social landing page aspect of this report, as it is one of the best ways to figure out which landing pages are best or worst when it comes to performance and engagement.

Acquisition Campaign Report

This is one of the most accurate and specific reports when it comes to traffic acquisition for your web property.

It is a centralized report highlighting campaigns from social, paid search, display and any tagged URL. You will also be able to see all URLs that you have UTM tagged.

What is a UTM tag? UTM stands for Urchin Tracking Module, but don't get caught up on the "Urchin" part. "Tracking Module" is what's relevant here. A UTM tag is a bit of code that you add to the end of a URL to track specific campaigns. If you were running a Facebook campaign, for example, you would add a UTM tag to all links used for that campaign, enabling you to track results. Without the tag, results from the campaign would be lumped in with all Facebook traffic and you would not be able to isolate them to accurately measure results.

- -

Takeaway

Understanding where your users are coming from and what they do once they arrive on your site provides incredibly valuable insight into how you can become even more useful and accessible. The data is there. Make it work for you.

Exercise:

Go to the Google Analytics Demo Account.

https://analytics.google.com/analytics/web/demoAccount

Complete the following exercises:
- Identify the traffic source with the highest level of engagement.
- Identify the source that is sending the most traffic to the site.
- Identify the top performing keywords.
- Identify the top performing social channel.

Chapter 25

Google Analytics & SEO

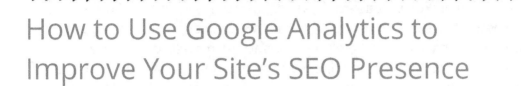

How to Use Google Analytics to Improve Your Site's SEO Presence

The Search Engine's Mission

The role of search engines is to crawl the web and index the pages that they deem worthy, in an order that provides value to users.

In doing so, their mission is to ensure users can quickly and easily find the information, products, services or content they're looking for.

Let's go back to Google's mission statement, written in 2013: "Google's mission is to organize the world's information and make it universally accessible and useful."

Source: *https://www.google.com/about/*

Bing's mission statement, also written in 2013, is as follows: "At Bing our central mission is to help you search less and do more. To that end, we're constantly looking for ways to make your search experience more efficient."

Source: https://blogs.bing.com/search/2013/08/23/find-it-faster-with-bing-product-search/

Yahoo's mission is to "make the world's daily habits inspiring and entertaining." Source: Yahoo.com

What can we take away from this?

Essentially, search engines exist to send us *away* from them and *to* what users search for. Ironic, isn't it?

Think about it. You visit a search engine, perform a search and then leave. The better the experience you have with a search engine (i.e. the greater success you have at finding what you want) the more likely you are to use that one again. With that in mind, you can rely on them wanting to return search results that are as closely related as possible to what it "thinks" you are truly looking for.

There is a lot to learn from this.

My grandpa used to say, "Tell me what someone wants and I will tell you how to control him." And I tell you today that if you want to control how your web property shows up in search engines, you have to understand that the primary mission of the search engine is around what people want and nothing else. Yes, the companies behind them want to make money through advertising, sales, etc., but they know that these things are most profitable when driven by that primary mission of providing value.

User driven metrics control search, and likely always will.

If you are able, through your site, to provide useful, accessible, engaging, inspiring and entertaining information, then you are golden. If people want you, search engines will want you. This should be the guiding principle behind your SEO strategy.

Thankfully, Google Analytics can help you understand what searchers want, like, enjoy, engage with and how you can act on that knowledge to improve your ranking.

Google Search Console on Google Analytics

Using Google Search Console and Google Analytics together empowers you to take a knowledge-driven approach to SEO.

To be able to make educated SEO decisions, you need Google Search Console. Once you connect Google Search Console data to your web property, you will have access to a wide array of reports that will help you understand how pages are performing, what keywords are sending the most traffic, what pages are getting the highest engagement, what is relevant and what is not. Combine that with GA and you get incredible insight into what people are doing after they click.

Let's jump into the GA dashboard (use the Demo account if you don't have GA set up yet).

Under "Acquisition" scroll to "Search Console". Without Google Search Console, the default analytics results are extremely limited. In fact, GA will often return "Not Provided".

With Search Console, you will have access to extensive data, which is enough to optimize, improve and plan ahead.

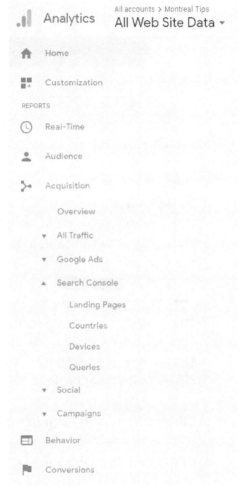

Also, Google Search Console is the best SEO tool out there that you can use for free. Make sure that you are using it and learning from it as much as possible.

Search Console Landing Pages Report

Landing Page	Acquisition					Behavior		Conversions Goal 1: Engaged Visitors ▾		
	Impressions ↓	Clicks	CTR	Average Position	Sessions	Bounce Rate	Pages / Session	Engaged Visitors (Goal 1 Completions)	Engaged Visitors (Goal 1 Value)	Engaged Visitors (Goal 1 Conversion Rate)
	72,718	3,584	4.93%	25	987	91.29%	1.23	29	CA$0.00	2.94%
	13,506	566	4.34%	30	203	93.10%	1.11	4	CA$0.00	1.97%
	12,350	579	4.69%	14	0	0.00%	0.00	0	CA$0.00	0.00%
	5,032	242	4.81%	35	96	93.75%	1.11	4	CA$0.00	4.17%
	3,904	76	1.95%	9.8	0	0.00%	0.00	0	CA$0.00	0.00%
	3,705	274	7.40%	25	152	92.76%	1.12	4	CA$0.00	2.63%

As you can see in the report above, GA provides a list of the most popular landing pages on your site that visitors have arrived at through organic search.

The table shows a lot of valuable info, which is the result of the merge between Google Search Console data and on-site behaviour data. This helps you not only know what people did to find your page, but what they did once they arrived there, and whether they took the actions that you want them to take.

━ ━

These are the terms you should know to get the most out of this report:

SERP (Search Engine Results Page) Impressions – This is the number of times your pages popped up in search results.

Clicks – The number of times people clicked on your page from an SERP.

CTR (Click Through Rate) – The number of clicks/the number of impressions * 100, meaning, it reflects the rate at which people see your listing in organic search results and choose to click through to your site.

Average Position – This is the average ranking of your page in organic search results, taking into account all the keywords that this page ranks for. If your page has an average position of 3, for example, that means your page usually shows up around the third spot in SERPs (which is a very good position to have).

Sessions – This is the number of visits that you get to your site from organic search.

Bounce Rate – This tells you how many visitors to your site (from organic search) left without taking any action.

Goal Metrics – This shows how your traffic from organic search is converting on the site.

The Landing Page Report gives you a view into how your different pages are performing from an SEO perspective. It helps you see what pages are performing well, which ones can be improved, and which pages you can capitalize on elsewhere, maybe through paid search or social campaigns.

Acquisition Google Search Console Countries Report

Country	Acquisition				B
	Impressions ↓	Clicks	CTR	Average Position	Sessions
	72,718 % of Total: 100.00% (72,718)	3,584 % of Total: 100.00% (3,584)	4.93% Avg for View: 4.93% (0.00%)	25 Avg for View: 25 (0.00%)	987 % of Total: 29.52% (3,344)
1. Canada	32,229 (44.32%)	1,991 (55.55%)	6.18%	14	500 (50.66%)
2. United States	12,661 (17.41%)	838 (23.38%)	6.62%	17	242 (24.52%)
3. India	3,828 (5.26%)	75 (2.09%)	1.96%	48	14 (1.42%)
4. United Kingdom	2,791 (3.84%)	197 (5.50%)	7.06%	18	60 (6.08%)
5. Brazil	1,250 (1.72%)	6 (0.17%)	0.48%	54	2 (0.20%)
6. Indonesia	1,022 (1.41%)	2 (0.06%)	0.20%	56	2 (0.20%)
7. France	915 (1.26%)	33 (0.92%)	3.61%	39	10 (1.01%)
8. Russia	900 (1.24%)	3 (0.08%)	0.33%	56	0 (0.00%)
9. Vietnam	875 (1.20%)	4 (0.11%)	0.46%	57	0 (0.00%)
10. Mexico	847 (1.16%)	17 (0.47%)	2.01%	37	10 (1.01%)

In this report, you can see the amount of organic search traffic you're getting from each country.

This insight can help you tailor future content for different countries, with different languages and different information that caters to specific audiences.

I use this report to understand who is coming to my site and how I can tailor new content for them. It also helps me identify opportunities I may be missing out on. For example, if I'm getting a lot of traffic from a specific country, but it isn't converting, I can start looking into why that may be, and what I can do to better serve that traffic and increase conversions.

In the sample report above, you can see that the US is the second biggest source of traffic to my site. Because of that, I try to tailor some content to that audience instead of only concentrating on Canadian traffic or local traffic.

Acquisition Google Search Console Device Report

Device Category	Acquisition				
	Impressions ↓	Clicks	CTR	Average Position	Sessions
	72,718 % of Total: 100.00% (72,718)	3,584 % of Total: 100.00% (3,584)	4.93% Avg for View: 4.93% (0.00%)	25 Avg for View: 25 (0.00%)	987 % of Total: 29.52% (3,344)
1. desktop	36,241 (49.84%)	1,507 (42.05%)	4.16%	37	758 (76.80%)
2. mobile	33,794 (46.47%)	1,846 (51.51%)	5.46%	13	95 (9.63%)
3. tablet	2,683 (3.69%)	231 (6.45%)	8.61%	8.9	134 (13.58%)

As small as this report is, it packs a big punch.

This gives you a quick overview of where you stand as a brand and site, as it shows your average position on mobile, tablet and desktop.

If you see that you have a lower than usual CTR on mobile, for example, it may be a sign that you are not appealing to users of these devices. You may find that you need to do a better job with meta title and meta descriptions, or even that your site isn't rendering properly on mobile devices.

Acquisition Google Search Console Queries Report

Search Query	Clicks	Impressions ↓	CTR	Average Position
	1,406 % of Total: 39.52% (3,970)	44,036 % of Total: 62.43% (70,931)	3.19% Avg for View: 3.97% (-37.20%)	32 Avg for View: 36 (38.11%)
1. national parks near montreal	123 (8.75%)	373 (0.85%)	32.98%	1.9
2. montreal national park	60 (4.37%)	196 (0.44%)	30.61%	1.9
3. national park near montreal	57 (4.09%)	119 (0.27%)	47.90%	1.5
4. indoor activities montreal	47 (3.34%)	730 (1.66%)	6.44%	7.0
5. montreal indoor activities	40 (2.84%)	368 (0.84%)	10.87%	5.2
6. montreal national parks	35 (2.49%)	99 (0.22%)	35.35%	1.7
7. national park montreal	28 (1.99%)	66 (0.12%)	42.42%	1.5
8. indoor activities in montreal	23 (1.64%)	136 (0.31%)	16.91%	4.3
9. best national parks near montreal	21 (1.49%)	39 (0.09%)	53.85%	1.3
10. canadian winter jackets brands	21 (3.49%)	597 (1.36%)	3.52%	11

This report is, for SEO purposes, the most important one in the Google Search Console reports, as it shows what terms and keywords visitors used to arrive on your site.

This shows what you're good at and what you can improve, in terms of keywords.

It is a great place to see what type of content to concentrate on more, and gives you the start of a model for how to approach future content and what types of terms to concentrate on for a more targeted and sustained approach to the details on your site.

Takeaway

Google Analytics, in partnership with Google Search Console, helps you understand how visitors search for your site, how they perceive it and if they find it relevant, giving you a starting point from which to build and improve on your content strategy for better SEO.

What makes GA so important as a tool, is that it taps into user metrics, and these user metrics are the main ranking factors of any website, as of this writing.

Exercise

Go to the Google Analytics Demo Account.

https://analytics.google.com/analytics/web/demoAccount

Complete the following exercises:
- Identify the terms driving the most organic traffic.
- Identify the terms driving the highest engagement.
- Identify the terms leading to the highest bounce rate.
- Identify the terms leading to the most conversions.
- Determine the average ranking position for branded terms (a branded term is one that includes the business or brand name).
- Identify the best performing landing page for organic traffic.

By extracting the information above, you will begin to build a picture of what is working, what is relevant and what should be optimized.

Chapter 26

SEO & SEM

>>>>>>>>>>>>>>>>>>>>>>>>>>>>>>>>>>>>>>>

SEM and SEO Have Always Complemented Each Other

My students always ask me which one they should concentrate on more: SEO or SEM?

The truth is, they both work together perfectly.

SEO impacts SEM and SEM impacts SEO.

Let's explore this.

In SEM - mainly with Bing Ads and Google Ads - there is a number called "quality score". The higher your quality score, the less you pay for clicks. It is Google's way of rewarding you for bringing value and being relevant. The way the quality score works is as follows: if your paid keyword is relevant to your ads, and both your ad and keyword are relevant to your landing page, you will have a higher quality score.

But, to have a relevant landing page, you need to have keywords and content on that page, and the page must be optimized accordingly. As for how SEM impact SEO, well it drives more traffic to the site, which in turn is the highest of SEO ranking factors.

As for how they work together... well, marketing is a bit of a turf war. The more turf you control, the more audience you will get. Meaning, if you are ranking #1 organically with SEO and #1 paid search with SEM, then you control a big chunk of that SERP. And what does that mean? It means users will have to take a few scrolls before they see the competition.

Always keep SEM in mind when working on your SEO. Use these two properly and it will multiply your wins.

Takeaway

When it comes to SEO and SEM, it isn't about which one to focus on more. It's about having them work together, complementing each other, and aligning with the full gamut of your digital marketing and business strategies.

Chapter 27

Google Analytics & Content

>>

How to Use Google Analytics to Create Better Content

Are You Missing the Boat on Data-Driven Content Marketing?

Do you want high performing content? We all want that!

In working with a variety of companies, from small start-ups to Fortune 500s, I've learned that Google Analytics is a tool not capitalized on enough, especially when it comes to content marketing. Even big companies, with huge marketing budgets, are missing the boat.

Interestingly, GA tends to be looked at only *after* a paid campaign, end of the season, or before the end of the year. Sadly, most companies don't even consider looking at data pre-campaign, which is a huge missed opportunity. The more I work with GA, the more I realize how necessary a research and study tool it is, and that it should be considered in all phases of a campaign, especially when it comes to content marketing.

Why? Because GA doesn't just tell you what worked, it can also help you predict what will work in the future and what to use to make it work... if you look in the right place!

That's why, when the time arrives to create relevant, engaging content, I look to five main GA metrics. A good grasp of these metrics is like a crystal ball view into giving users more of what they want.

- **Site Content**

In GA, just under "Site Content", you can see the pages on your site that get the most visits. This provides insight into your most popular topics or content types, allowing you to predict the topics and formats that are most engaging and appealing to your visitors.

Look at your bounce rates, exits and average time on page. With this data, you will be able to plan future content either by using similar content structure, similar topics, or even just a similar general approach.

- **Site Search**

If you have Site Search capabilities built in, Site Search metrics is the best way to see what people look for once they arrive on your site.

Are people searching for something you don't have a lot of content on? Or maybe you do, but they're using different terms and not finding what you have?

Remember, knowing what people are looking for is like having a crystal ball, telling you what content to create or enhance.

This can tell you how to cater to new visitors, align your content strategy with current customer needs, and know what content to use in ads and promotions. Basically, it tells you how to be more useful and accessible.

- **Audience Details**

What type of people are visiting your site? This can help you determine the type of content to deliver. For example, you may discover you have a large millennial or baby boomer audience you can tailor content to. Perhaps you have high traffic from a particular country and you can adjust some existing content to have a more local flair.

When it comes to audience details, there can be many factors to consider. To make better sense of the numbers, I usually look at minimum 3 months of data to get more content-worthy metrics, and look at these key metrics:

1. Demographics (age and gender)
2. Interests (affinity categories and in-market segments) - Helps me understand the general and related interests that my visitors have, allowing me to create better content and target them in my social or search campaigns.
3. Geo (language and location) - Pay close attention to language. Over time, you may notice a growing traffic segment associated with another language, or that there is potential for expanding your market.

Having this demographic knowledge will help you create the right content, for the right age group, at the right place, at the right time.

- **Channels**

'Acquisition' is the way in which you acquire visitors. 'Channels' refers to your acquisition channels - the sources driving visitors. This is where you will find the top sources of traffic to your site. For example, you can acquire visitors from Google, referrals from other sites, article mentions, newsletters and more.

Knowing how you got your current visitors will help you understand how your content is being shared, searched and viewed, and which content is best at drawing people in.

Knowing this empowers you to create content catered to the different visitors in your different channels, and create even more of the type of content that is best at bringing new visitors to your site.

- **Search Console**

As we looked at earlier, under 'Acquisition' in GA is where you'll find your Search Console data, which, as previously discussed, is only functional when you link GA with Google Search Console.

From Search Console, you can see which keywords or queries in Google are leading people to your site. You will also see how well you rank for these keywords, and the number of impressions you get for them.

This data will allow you to assess what is working as far as search goes, help you further capitalize on these topics, and empower you to work on better and more relevant content for your site.

Takeaway

Analytics can be a big part of creating great content, which is a critical element of great SEO. Taking advantage of Analytics BEFORE creating or modifying content makes it part of a truly powerful cycle of creating content, seeing how it works on your web properties and sites, realigning your content strategy in accordance with the data gathered, and back to creating content. The big difference being, your content gets better, more relevant and more engaging each time.

Make sure you are using GA to its fullest potential and your fullest advantage. Always check your data and analytics before planning strategies or campaigns. Listen to what they are telling you. Make them an essential part of your overall marketing strategy and you will begin to see your content performing better than ever before.

Exercise:

Consider your ideal target market and create 2 or 3 detailed personas of specific (hypothetical) people you are targeting. What's their age range? Profession? Lifestyle? Interests? Shopping habits? Search habits?

Now, using those personas, create content! Write one paragraph of targeted content for each persona that aligns fully with the persona details. For the sake of this exercise, assume that you are selling Google merchandise on the Google Merchandise store.

https://www.googlemerchandisestore.com/

If you're finding it difficult to write for the personas you created, resist the urge to create new personas. In the real world, you get the visitors you get. Consider this good practice and a valuable workout for your creative muscles.

Chapter 28

Google Analytics & SEM

>>

SEM Stands for Search Engine Marketing

Both SEO and SEM fall under the search marketing umbrella. SEO is the organic traffic and SEM is the paid traffic. We've already discussed how SEO and SEM can work together, so let's now take a dive into SEM and how to drive the greatest benefit from it.

The tools that most advertisers use to run SEM campaigns are Google Ads and Bing Ads.

For the sake of this book, we will take a peek into how Google Ads works with Google Analytics, highlight the value of these two tools working together, and explore how to use the resulting reports and data.

One big benefit of using GA is that it is easily integrated with other Google tools. This seamless integration is a big advantage when it comes to data. Google Ads is by far one of the most superior tools when it comes to creating search, video and display campaigns. Yet, on its own, it's not enough.

Any marketer with knowledge of the ad industry will tell you that without integrating Google Ads with Google Analytics, you can't fully capitalize on the tool.

Alone, Google Ads can give you insight into how users are performing before they arrive on your site, but the moment they arrive on your site, Google Ads tracking is done. That's where you want Analytics to pick up the thread, as it is critical to understand what your ad traffic does post-click. This is how you know whether or not the investments you're making are worth it.

Integrating GA with Google Ads will allow you to get the full picture so that you can respond accordingly.

To get started, we need to connect our GA account with Google Ads.

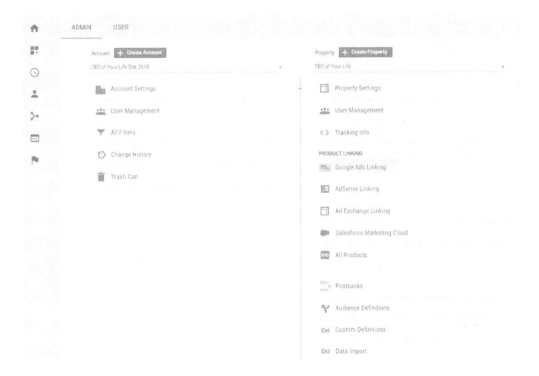

Go to Admin in your GA account. Under "Property" select "Google Ads Linking". You'll then get a window asking you to add a new link group.

Click "New Link Group" and a window will pop up showing you all the Google Ads accounts you are running under your associated Gmail account (remember that it all starts with a Gmail address).

If you are running a Google Ads account under another Gmail address, it might be best to transfer ownership so that you can make the connection.

Select the account you want to connect and click "Continue".

You will then be asked to add a link group title, connect to a specific view and hit "Save".

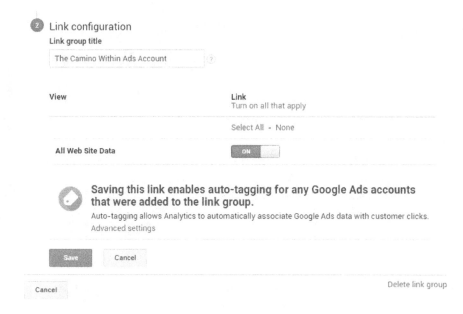

This connection will bring a lot of benefits, whether it's the more in-depth reporting from the Google Analytics side of things, or the ability to customize your bidding and targeting based on the data that you are extracting to Google Ads.

So, if we go to the main Analytics report section in GA, click on "Acquisition" and scroll to "Google Ads", a drop down will show up. Here's what to pay attention to:

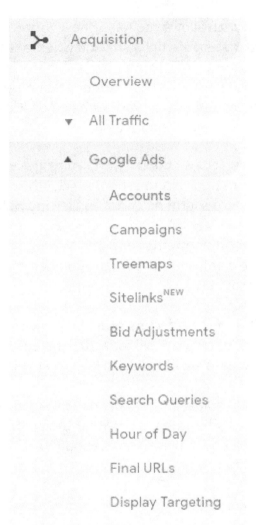

Accounts: this report shows you how your account is performing and, if you have more than one account connected, it will allow you to see how the accounts are performing compared to each other.

For most of the companies I work with, there is usually one account. The main benefit of this report is that you are able to see the performance of the whole account in one place. Meaning, if there is any drop, spike, or problem, it is easy to pinpoint.

Also, this report gives you a quick idea of whether your investment is worth it and if you might want to invest more, depending on your budget.

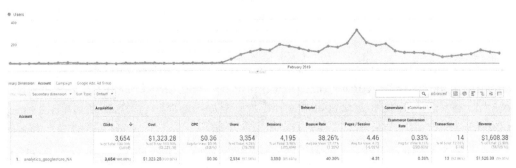

The reason I say this is due to the fact that you can see clicks, visits, behaviour and conversions all in one place.

The second tab to look at is the **Campaigns** tab.

This tab allows you to see how your campaigns are performing, how visitors to the site are behaving and whether they are converting.

The **Sitelinks** tab is another great report as it gives an in-depth look into which sitelinks on your Google Ads account are the best performers, and what you can improve on.

When I look at this report, I'm typically searching for the most successful terms and calls to action, which I then use to improve any ads that are underperforming or not converting well.

Bid Adjustments report:
A bid adjustment is when you alter your bid for certain factors in your Ads account.

One of these factors could be device (Mobile, Computer or Tablet). Let's say you adjust your bid for a 10% increase on mobile. As you would expect, this increase should (ideally) lead to an increase in leads, impressions and clicks.

A bid adjustment can be either negative or positive. For example, I could set a bid adjustment of -10% for tablet, meaning we would likely see a drop-in tablet ad impressions of about 10%.

Campaign	Device	Bid Adj.	Acquisition			Behavior				Conversions eCommerce ▾		
			Clicks ↓	Cost	CPC	Users	Sessions	Bounce Rate	Pages / Session	Ecommerce Conversion Rate	Transactions	Revenue
	ALL	--	3,654	$1,323.28	$0.36	2,934	3,593	40.30%	4.31	0.36%	13	$1,528.39
1 ▾ AW - Apparel	ALL	--	1,556	$380.53	$0.25	1,244	1,617	27.83%	5.42	0.96%	9	$1,277.91
	Computers	--	858	$327.62	$0.38	686	871	27.21%	5.35	0.23%	2	$64.97
	Mobile devices with full browsers	--	660	$59.86	$0.09	521	703	29.02%	5.40	0.95%	6	$1,151.97
	Tablets with full browsers	--	49	$2.95	$0.06	36	43	20.93%	7.28	2.33%	1	$61.77
2 ▸ AW - YouTube	ALL	--	1,395	$678.44	$0.50	1,100	1,175	62.81%	2.17	0.00%	0	$0.00
3 ▸ AW - Google Brand	ALL	--	321	$101.99	$0.32	273	368	36.16%	4.39	0.58%	2	$94.55

The Bid Adjustment report helps you see whether the adjustments you make are yielding better results or leading to a higher ROI. And, if not, it might be a good idea to revisit the bid adjustment that you set up in the first place.

Keywords and Search Queries reports are two different reports. The Keywords report shows you which keywords you input into Google Ads and how they are performing. The Search Queries report shows you the keywords used by search engine users that led them to your site or web property.

Final URLs Report is a great one to look at. This shows you which of your landing pages are performing best. You can act on that insight by using your top performing landing pages more often, or by taking elements of your successful landing pages and repeating them on others to improve their performance.

Hour of Day Report shows you the best performing hours of the day. This is helpful because time of day is one of the metrics you can set when setting up your bids. Ideally, you want to concentrate your investment on the hours that perform best for you.

━ ━

Google Ads

Google Analytics and Google Ads, when used together, have even more benefits you can tap into from the Google Ads side.

- **Goals and Conversions.**
When connecting the two accounts together, you will be able to import your goals from Google Analytics into Google AdWords, meaning you will be able to optimize your campaigns to goals and acquisitions, vs. just clicks and impressions.

- **CPA– Cost per acquisition**
When you have AdWords connected to Analytics, you will be able to start using the CPA bidding strategy, instead of just CPC (Cost Per Click) and CPM (Cost per 1000 Impressions). This matters because while clicks and impressions are important to measure, whether or not those clicks and impressions lead to actual visits matters more.

- **Audiences & Remarketing**
Google Analytics allows you to create audiences which you can then target in your Google Ads. Here's how you set it up:

- Go to the admin section in GA.
- Under "Property", click on "Audience Definitions", then "Audiences".
- This is where you can create an audience, then export it to your Google Ads account, where you can target a specific group of users, with specific ads. (This is also called remarketing.)

To create the audience:

- Click "New Audience" under the audience settings.
- Select the view that you want to create the audience under and click "Next".

Click "Create New" and an audience creation window will pop up, allowing you to filter out an audience you want to target. See example below:

Click "Apply" and you will be prompted to name the audience. Name it something relevant as you will use it on Google Ads later. Click "Next Step".

The last step is to choose where you want to publish this audience. I recommend choosing Google Analytics and Google Ads.

This will help you see the performance of the audience on both Google Analytics and Google Ads. Keep in mind that "Publish" does not mean you're making anything public. It just means you're granting access to the tools you choose - in this example, GA and Google Ads - so that you will be able to see the data and reporting in those tools.

Takeaway

Google Analytics and Google Ads can be fully integrated, which provides you with incredibly valuable and actionable insights, allowing you to optimize your SEM efforts in a way that complements your SEO. Make sure you are capitalizing on this integration from both tools.

Exercise:

Connect your Google Analytics account to your Google AdWords account. Create an audience in GA and export it to Google Ads.

Chapter 29

Google Optimizer & AB Testing

>>

Testing is What Makes Marketing Work

Marketing is not supposed to work the first time around

When it comes to all aspects of marketing, and especially SEO, analytics is your greatest weapon and tool. Ideally, it should be the focus of about ⅔ of your efforts. Why? It shows if, and how well, your efforts are working, it gives you a baseline to start from and identify what you need to work on, it provides insight into the opportunities available to you, and so much more. Essentially, it tells you where you are, where you need to go, and what you need to work on to get there. And, possibly the best tool to use for analytics is GA (sure helps that it's free, too).

How should you be spending that recommended ⅔? On research, implementation and reporting/testing.

We've already gone through different methods of researching and implementation. Let's now look at testing.

Google Optimizer is what you will use for testing. It is the best way to see and test what is working and what is not working, so that you can optimize accordingly.

"Engage your website visitors like never before. Create personalized experiences and test what works best — for free."

Google Optimize

To get started with Google Optimizer, go to:
https://marketingplatform.google.com/about/optimize/

You will be sent to the Google Optimizer Dashboard, where you click "Create Experience".

Experience means the experience you are creating for visitors to interact with. It is the experience that you'll be testing.

Once you click "Create", a new experience sidebar will pop up:

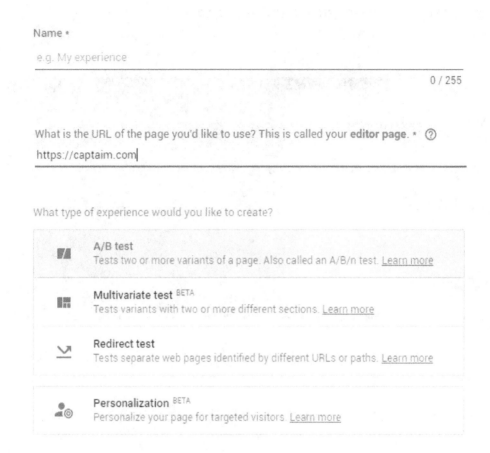

To start:

First step: Enter the name of the experience you want to create.

- Be descriptive and specific as you will be creating a lot of these experiences in the future.
- As a best practice, I tend to include the start date, the purpose and the type of experience. For example, "21st March 2019 Cap.TaiM – Redirect Test".

The second step is to add your URL. This is the URL of the page that you want to use for this experiment. In this example, I'm using my homepage, https://captaim.com.

The third step is to specify which type of experiment you want to run.

- **A/B Test -** Tests two or more variants of a page. Also called an A/B/n test.
- **Multivariate test -** Tests variants with two or more different sections.
- **Redirect Test -** Tests separate web pages identified by different URLs or paths.
- **Personalization -** Personalize your page for targeted visitors.

Source: Google Optimizer: https://optimize.google.com/

For this example, I will choose the redirect test. This is perfect for testing things like which contact page will work best, to see if it is better to send people to your workshop page or book page, or some other similar test.

For this example, I will be testing my workshop page vs. my book page to see which will perform best:

https://captaim.com/workshops/ or **https://captaim.com/book/**

To get started, choose the variant.

The two pages I am testing are each a variant in the test, so I will create one variant for each, as well as my original, which is my homepage:

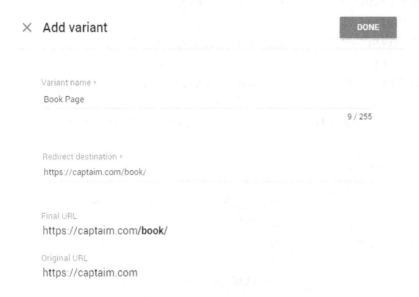

As you can see, all the variants have been added:

I'll next add a description:

Optimize

📈 Measurement and objectives

📊 Google Analytics
Optimize uses Google Analytics for measurement.

Link to your Google Analytics property to enable measurement.

LINK TO ANALYTICS

🚩 Objectives ⑦
The website functionality you wish to optimize. Learn more

Before adding objectives, you need to link this container and experience to Analytics.

There isn't much point in running a test if we can't analyze results, so my next step is to connect Google Optimize with GA.

I will also activate email notifications to receive the most important and relevant updates.

When all is set, I'll click "Start" to kick off the experiment.

Takeaway

Testing is essential to know what is working, what is not and where to make changes or adjustments. This insight allows us to continually improve the usefulness and accessibility of our sites and their content, thereby strengthening our SEO efforts.

Make sure to tap into the different types of testing that Google provides and make sure that you are using them to your advantage.

Exercise

Create a Google Optimizer Account and launch an experiment that you deem relevant for your business. When deciding what's relevant for your business, remember to think in terms of optimizing the user experience. And don't forget to connect Optimizer to GA.

Bonus Chapter
Dealing with SEO Experts and Agencies.

Questions Businesses Should Ask BEFORE Signing an Agency Contract

10 Questions Every Business Should Ask Before Kicking Off an SEO Project

People often come to me asking what they should ask their agency before they get the agency started on their site SEO. This, itself, is a really important question. And I always say that it depends on the specific circumstances. But, there are some basic questions that should be asked by all businesses before engaging an agency in this type of project.

Before we start with the list, it's important to know that getting an external person or agency to do your SEO is like giving them the keys to your backdoor. It is important that you trust that person, or that the company is of high authority in the market.

One thing that frightens me is when I do SEO for a client and discover that the person who did their SEO previously left some backlinks for other clients he or she was working with. Not only is this illegal, it will also negatively impact your site authority and can cause a drop in SEO strength. That's pretty much the opposite of what you want.

Given the impact this person or agency can have, **it is so important for you to know that you are dealing with the right person.**

So, let's dig into the main questions you should ask your SEO agency BEFORE giving them the keys:

1. What is the most recent Google algorithm update, what should I be considering when it comes to my site, and how many algorithm updates happen annually? An expert should be able to answer this with confidence.

2. What process will you follow when it comes to optimization? The brief answer should be something along the lines of:

    1. Audit
    2. Meeting
    3. Recommendations
    4. Optimizations

    You don't want someone going cowboy on you and jumping to #4 while skipping some, or even all, of the previous steps.

3. Can you give me a list of the keywords you have optimized for and what you ranked for?
    They should be able to give you real world examples of what they've worked on (either for their own projects or, ideally, work they've done for clients).

4. When will I start seeing results?
    The best answer should be 5 to 10 months, depending on the size of the site and the level of competition in that industry.

5. Who will be implementing the optimization?
    It is preferable that you do your own optimization, especially if it is your first interaction with this agency.

    On the other hand, the option of having the agency implement optimizations will ensure full liability on them, and ensure that everything is done professionally.

    It is your call on this one.

6. **Do you align SEO strategy with content strategy?** (The answer should be yes.)

7. **Do you align SEO strategy with social strategy?** (Should be yes.)

8. **Do you address both off-page and on-page optimization?** (Again, should be yes.)

9. **How often will the agency be updating me?**

10. **Who will be responsible for reporting?**

Even if this back and forth is brief, it will show the agency that you know what you are doing and what to expect. Their answers will also give you a feeling of if the agency is professional, respectful and knows what they're doing. Don't be afraid to also ask for references and to check those references.

Finally, and most importantly, make sure that you have a proper scope of work and a quote that matches it.

Source/Reference:
http://www.searchenginejournal.com/20-questions-to-ask-before-you-hire-an-seo-agency-in-post-pandapenguin-era/62504/

Takeaway

Depending on your area of expertise and/or resources, it can make sense to hire an external contractor or agency to handle your SEO. But handing over your SEO is like handing over the keys to your house. Trust is probably the most important element of the relationship. Take the time to educate yourself about SEO basics (like reading this book!) so that you can get a good idea if they know what they're talking about, and don't hesitate to ask as many questions as you need to before signing a contract.

Book Takeaways

- Make "useful and accessible" your mantra - in SEO and in all aspects of digital marketing.
- SEO doesn't work on its own, it works as part of a digital marketing mix. SEO only exists and improves when all digital marketing channels are working together in the most holistic manner possible.
- There are no guarantees in SEO, nor is there a silver bullet.
- SEO requires a lot of hard work and consistent efforts to get the right results.
- The most important ranking factors in SEO and for search engines are user behavior metrics and user engagement. Optimize with the user in mind first.
- Align, align, align! SEO is one part of your overall business and marketing machine. Align your strategies and take all players into account.
- Black hat tactics are not good business. Stick to white hat if your goal is long term results with good conversion rates.
- Content is still one of the most important factors in SEO, and will continue to drive value in years to come.
- To capitalize on intent, pay attention to the four types of queries: informational, investigative, navigational and transactional.
- Search is all about finding good, relevant, accessible content.
- SEO and content marketing are allies. Make yours work together.
- Capitalize on your off-season to build and maintain strong search rankings.
- Keywords still matter (a lot), but they must be used strategically. Do your research!
- Don't neglect indirect impacts. Things like image alt tags and meta titles may no longer have direct SEO impact, but do impact user behaviour, which impacts SEO success.
- For a successful site migration, be vigilant in all 3 phases: pre-migration, migration and post-migration.
- Use Google Analytics and set it up BEFORE starting on SEO so you have a baseline for tracking progress.
- SEO doesn't only bring value to your organic campaigns, but to paid search campaigns as well.
- Google is not the only search engine out there. We need to optimize for all the search engines in the market or we miss out on a big chunk of it.

- Site structure is extremely important for SEO. A well-structured site will help with the short and the long-term SEO strength of the site.
- Site structure includes keyword mapping, content structure and URL structure.
- Page structure is extremely important for SEO as well, as it will help dictate how the tags will be implemented and the flow on the page.
- Page speed matters. As our collective attention span is getting shorter and shorter, we will continue to have huge bounce rates associated with low page speed. Optimizing your page speed will lead to better user engagement, lower bounce rate and, eventually, better ranking.
- Clean your code. A site with clean code takes less time to load and loads smoothly - for the user AND the search engines. Bear that in mind as part of your optimization.
- Mobile friendliness and site responsiveness are extremely important for SEO and user engagement across mobile.
- If you have made no major changes and your rankings start to drop, the first place to look is site performance.
- Take advantage of your data and use the tools Google provides to analyze it, derive meaningful insights, and optimize.
- SEO and SEM work best when they work together. Align your efforts.
- If running an SEM campaign through Google Ads, be sure to connect your Ads account to your Google Analytics account to derive the most valuable insights.
- Testing is key. Use Google Optimize to test, analyze, optimize, repeat.
- Bring value. If the site is not bringing value, then there is no point in it ranking on search engines, or existing for that purpose.
- Voice search and questions. The way we search is changing and we are relying on voice search more and more. We are also searching more with a query in mind, rather than just a statement. This affects SEO. Strongly.
- If hiring an agency or outside contractor to handle your SEO, trust is key. Educate yourself. Ask questions. Be vigilant.

References:

General Reference:
https://datastudio.google.com
https://analytics.google.com

The data used in the Analytics reports contained in this book is derived from three accounts:
- Montrealtips.com
- Google Demo Account
- Google Merchandise Store

Reference by Chapter:

Chapter 8:
https://moz.com/blog/segmenting-search-intent
http://searchengineland.com/search-intent-signals-aligning-organic-paid-search-strategy-249601

Chapter 8.1:
Resources/Sources:
https://blog.kissmetrics.com/seo-is-content-marketing/
http://www.searchenginejournal.com/combine-seo-content-marketing-explosive-results/97157/
http://searchengineland.com/content-marketing-seo-bigger-picture-219796
http://www.searchenginejournal.com/combine-seo-content-marketing-explosive-results/97157/

Chapter 9:
Google My Business – https://www.google.com/business/
Bing Places – https://www.bingplaces.com
Yelp – https://biz.yelp.com
Yellow Pages – http://m1.adsolutions.yp.com/free-listing-basic-benefits
FourSquare – http://business.foursquare.com
Whitepages – https://www.whitepages.com

Chapter 12:
https://moz.com/learn/seo/title-tag

Chapter 13:
https://moz.com/blog/web-site-migration-guide-tips-for-seos
http://searchengineland.com/seo-strategy-during-website-redesign-or-migration-221339

Chapter 14: https://smallseotools.com/code-to-text-ratio-checker/
https://validator.w3.org/
https://www.semrush.com/

Chapter 15: https://analytics.google.com/analytics/web/demoAccount

Chapter 16: https://developers.google.com/speed/pagespeed/insights/

Chapter 17:
https://yoast.com/site-structure-the-ultimate-guide/#why-important
https://moz.com/learn/seo/internal-link

Chapter 18: https://search.google.com/search-console/mobile-friendly
https://developers.google.com/speed/pagespeed/insights/

Chapter 25: https://blogs.bing.com/search/2013/08/23/find-it-faster-with-bing-product-search/

Chapter 27: https://www.googlemerchandisestore.com/

About the Author

Tarek Riman is Founder of Cap.TaiM, a full-service digital marketing agency (Captaim.com), Montreal Tips (Montrealtips.com) and Inspiring Canadians (inspiringcanadians.com). He is an entrepreneur, philanthropist, university professor and the bestselling author of *The Secret to Capitalizing on Analytics* and *The Camino Within*.

Tarek has worked with hundreds of agencies, SMBs and Fortune 500s, and holds over 30 digital marketing certifications. He is also a contributor to Thrive Global, Huffington Post, Social Media Today and has been featured on Breakfast Television, MTV Lebanon, and Change It Up Radio California. Tarek helps NGOs, students, associations and causes around the world. He has a fund in his name in Lebanon to educate students in need, and donated the proceeds of his first 200 books to the UNHCR. The proceeds of his blog, Montreal Tips, go to the Montreal Children's Hospital.

As a business speaker, he gives workshops and presentations on topics such as Analytics for Businesses and Entrepreneurs, SEO for Entrepreneurs, Digital Marketing for businesses, and Content Marketing. As a motivational speaker, he gives presentations based on his book, *The Camino Within*, which includes topics such as Preparing for the Camino, Transitioning and Breaking Out of Your Comfort Zone.

Tarek Riman's Digital Certifications

Google AdWords Certifications

- Google Advanced Search
- Advertising Fundamentals
- Mobile Advertising
- Video Advertising
- Shopping Advertising
- Display Advertising
- Accredited Bing Ads Professional
- Google Tag Manager
- DoubleClick Rich Media

Google Analytics Certifications

- Google Analytics Certified Individual
- Digital Analytics Fundamentals
- Platform Principles
- Ecommerce Analytics
- Mobile App Analytics
- Advanced Google Analytics
- Google Analytics for Beginners
- Google Mobile Site
- Google Digital Sales

Facebook Certifications

- Targeting: Core Audiences Certification
- FB & Instagram Certification
- Promote Your Business from Your FB Page Certification
- Ad Auction & Delivery Overview
- Extend Your Campaign's Reach with Audience Network

Other Certifications

- Google Wildfire
- Woorank | Certified Marketing Partner
- Hootsuite Certified Professional
- HubSpot | Inbound Marketing Certified
- SEMrush SEO Certified

The Secret To Capitalizing On Analytics

An Analytics book by Tarek Riman

The Secret to Capitalizing on Analytics' purpose is to help start-ups, students, beginners and entrepreneurs understand how to use data to optimize and improve their business and marketing strategies. All businesses today, no matter what their size, need to know how their website is performing. Without analytics, there is no way for a company to know how their website is performing in terms of attracting, informing and converting visitors.

In this book, you will learn how to get started with Google Analytics and how to set it up for optimal tracking. You will also learn to assess which marketing campaigns bring the best traffic to your website, which pages on your website are the most popular and how to extract information about your visitors. Information such as location, interests, age, behaviours and more so you can better understand your web traffic and capitalize on your marketing. You will also learn how to capitalize on the different trends and tools that are available.

The Camino Within

A life book by Tarek Riman

Learn more about Tarek through his first book, The Camino Within

The Camino Within summary:

Have you ever felt that what you do is a reflection of what you've been taught and not a true reflection of who you are?

Have you ever felt that you've fast-forwarded through life, or have lived it on autopilot, just doing what's expected of you?

If you were to leave all your successes and possessions behind to explore beyond your comfort zone, what would you find?

Perhaps most importantly, what can you do today to become more alive in all your tomorrows?

Trek along with Tarek on his pilgrimage of physical and emotional endurance, of blistered feet and broken bikes, of the meeting of unlikely souls, and the generosity of some inspiring people he met along the way.

In The Camino Within, Tarek Riman takes you on an adventure through 500 miles of the Camino de Santiago, leading you to many insightful revelations he picked up along the way and brought home with him to stay.

Tarek will inspire you to intentionally and actively reflect on the stories you tell yourself, so that you can take your own personal Camino Within. He did this work by literally leaving everything behind: comfort, material possessions, technology, employment and important relationships! By breaking out of convention, he fueled his own personal growth, through which he provides key takeaways in every chapter to help inspire you to face your own personal challenges and aspirations. The Camino Within promises readers an engaging read that can give rise to adventures of the soul and a more meaningful life.

This book will help you question your beliefs in order to understand, once and for all, if they are truly yours. It will help you see how powerful and cleansing such a journey can be, begin to uncover your own deep truths, and lead you to discover who you truly are.

To learn more about the book, check out thecaminowithin.com

LET'S STAY IN TOUCH

To stay updated on Tarek Riman's adventures, marketing for businesses, or Montreal Tips, you can follow him on Instagram at @taou, or check out his websites:

The Camino Within Book Site: https://thecaminowithin.com
The Secret to Capitalizing on Analytics Site: https://captaim.com/book
The SEO Way Site: https://captaim.com/seo-book
Email Tarek: triman@captaim.com
Connect with Tarek Riman on LinkedIn:
https://www.linkedin.com/in/tarekriman/
Twitter: @tarekriman
Instagram: @taou

CPSIA information can be obtained
at www.ICGtesting.com
Printed in the USA
LVHW101702260819
628959LV00009B/515/P